MINISTERS OF THE
FREE NORTH CHURCH, INVERNESS
1843-1974

Ministers of the Free North Church, Inverness

1843-1974

Hugh M Ferrier

Scottish Reformed Heritage Publications
2022

ISBN: 978-1-4717-1984-4

Front Cover:

Free North, Free Church of Scotland building in Inverness, from across the River Ness. The building was opened on 7th June 1893.

(Photo by John W Keddie).

Publisher:
Scottish Reformed Heritage Publications
19 Newton Park
Kirkhill
Inverness-shire
IV5 7QB

CONTENTS

FOREWORD

MY HUSBAND had hoped to see a book published on the ministers who preceded him in the Free North, but illness overtook him before he completed it.

He had a little information about the late Rev. James Fraser from his second wife, Mrs Mabel Fraser. I asked Mr Fraser's son, Donald, if he would be good enough to enlarge on that, which he did. As he was a student in Edinburgh much of the time when his father was in the Free North, Donald said that he could not write at length on his father's time there, and he suggested that Mr Sandy Finlay might write something regarding those years. I am very grateful to Donald and to Sandy for what they have done, because I felt that it would be a great pity if my dear husband's labour of love would remain unpublished.

I am greatly indebted, as Hugh also was, to Mrs Janet Munro for her invaluable help in typing up all the papers on her computer, and to the Rev. John Keddie for his much-appreciated assistance regarding the publishing of the book.

Georet Ferrier
Inverness
January 2022

MINISTERS OF THE FREE NORTH CHURCH, INVERNESS

1843-1974

Rev Archibald Cook 1843 – 1844

Rev George Mackay 1845 – 1886

Rev Murdo Mackenzie 1887 – 1912

Rev John Macleod 1913 – 1930

Rev Kenneth Cameron 1930 – 1945

Rev Donald Campbell 1951 – 1967

Rev James Fraser 1968 – 1974

CHAPTER 1

ARCHIBALD COOK

THE COOK BROTHERS were born at Achariach, Glen Scoridale, in south Arran. Their father was a tenant farmer who had married a Margaret MacBride. They had a family of nine sons. Finlay the third of them was born in 1778 and Archibald, the seventh, was born in 1789.

We know little of the boys' early life in Arran except that in a beautiful and unspoiled setting they grew up close to nature. In early life they came under conviction of sin through the powerful preaching of their minister the Rev. Neil MacBride and they were led to faith in Christ. In his unconverted days, Finlay was a proud and frivolous young man and when the Kilmory revival began, his main reason for attending church was to satisfy his curiosity by viewing what was happening and making fun of the proceedings. Donald Sage in his *Memorabilia Domestica* wrote that, "Mr. Cook had been one of the most thoughtless, light-headed young men in the island; indeed, he was in the act of jibing and mocking the venerable servant of God, in his pew in the church, when the arrows of Divine truth smote him. From that momentous hour he ceased to mock and began to pray."[1]

---

[1] Donald Sage, *Memorabilia Domestica*, Wick, ²1889, p. 285.

Archibald was of a more serious cast of mind, and in order to lift his spirits some of his companions introduced him to a dancing school on the island but this only served to have the opposite effect. His aversion to dancing remained with him throughout life. What affected Archie Cook was the faithful and rousing preaching of Neil MacBride. Through that preaching he saw, as never before, his desperate need as a sinner and that his only hope was in Christ Jesus the Saviour. Like his brother Finlay, he, too, gladly committed his life to the Lord.

Rev. Archibald Cook. First minister of the North Church in Inverness (1837), and afterwards the Free North (from 1843).

Both brothers felt called to preach the gospel and eventually they were accepted as candidates for the ministry. Although seriously disadvantaged as far as education and financial means were concerned, they proceeded to Glasgow to study at the University. In those days the course for the ministry lasted eight years and sometimes more. Finlay, being the older, went first and in Glasgow he made the acquaintance of Dr John Love, minister of Anderston Street Church of Scotland, and Dr Robert Balfour minister of the Cathedral. These were the two outstanding evangelical preachers in the city. Some years later Archie followed his brother and for two sessions during their studies they shared the same lodgings.

In a biographical sketch written in the early part of the twentieth century, Professor J. R. Mackay records a time when the brothers were in great poverty, and Archie had serious thoughts about giving up his studies in order for Finlay to continue. They prayed about the matter and one day after pouring out their hearts to God in great earnestness they had scarcely risen from their knees "when a knock was heard at the door of their room, and there entered a lady and gentleman, utter strangers to them, who gave them, one £4 and the other £5. After this deliverance they never found themselves again in financial straits."[2] The two young men thanked God and took courage and proved from then on that the Heavenly Father who feeds the ravens and clothes the lilies looks after those who trust in him.

Their intellectual gifts were no more than average but by steady application they achieved their goal, and in 1816 Finlay was licensed to preach the gospel by the Presbytery of Lanark, and in 1822 Archie was licensed by the Presbytery of Glasgow. In God's Providence these men were destined to minister in Inverness and to make a spiritual impact upon the Highlands in general, so that even today their names are not forgotten by lovers of the old paths. We consider, first of all, Finlay Cook's contribution as a preacher.

During his summer vacations as a student, he was employed as a missionary by Robert Owen at the Lanark cotton mills. Owen was a visionary and a reformer who sought to uplift and help socially deprived people. At the beginning of his work he was predisposed towards religion but his 'socialism' led to secularism and eventually Owen became a believer in 'spiritism.' But the experience that Cook acquired at the mills was invaluable. There he saw the obvious need of people spiritually and materially, and he could not but admire Owen's efforts to ease their plight and alleviate their poverty. After student days, Finlay Cook was ordained to the ministry in 1817 and thereafter inducted to the Achrenny Mission in Caithness, and here he came into contact with 'The Separatists.' Cook won their confidence by the deep spirituality of his life and by his sound preaching of the gospel. Later on, he was to acknowledge that some of his happiest days were spent at Achrenny. His friendship with Donald Sage who lived at his father's manse at Kildonan, brought about Finlay's acquaintance with Sage's sister, Elizabeth. They were eventually married in 1819 in her father's manse in Kildonan. They had three children, two

---

[2] J. R. Mackay (ed.), *Sermons in Gaelic and English by Rev. A. Cook*, Glasgow, 1907, p. xvii.

of whom died in infancy. The surviving son, Alexander, became the highly esteemed Free Church minister of Stratherrick. He was a young man of superior intelligence who would have gone far had he been spared, but he died in 1862 at the early age of thirty-seven. The type of man that he was can be gauged by a booklet he wrote, called *The Afflicted Christian Cottager*, the life of a fine Christian woman called Ealasaid Ruadh, or Red Elizabeth.

In 1829 Finlay Cook was called to Cross in Lewis and, although his ministry there was of short duration, he left behind him a lasting impression on the Lewis people. In his book, *Aspects of the Religious History of Lewis*, the Rev. Murdo Macaulay records the following assessment made by one of Cook's admirers: "I have known men quite as godly as he was, perhaps some even more so, but Mr Cook was one of the most godly I have ever known. I have heard men who could preach as well as he could, some perhaps even better, but he was one of the best preachers I have ever heard. I have seen some men who could catechize as well as he, some perhaps even better, but he was one of the best catechists I have ever seen. I have seen men who could manage a congregation as well as he could, but he was about the best for managing a congregation I have ever seen. So when I take all things together, I have not seen another like him as an all-round minister of the gospel."[3] That is praise indeed.

In 1833 he was called to the Chapel of Ease on Academy Street in Inverness. This Church was later named the East Church. The name 'Chapels of Ease' was given to churches which the Church of Scotland allowed people to build in order to call a minister of their own choice without interference from a patron. These churches had no ecclesiastical status, and their ministers had no Presbyterial responsibilities, nor could the ministers take part in Presbytery decisions. When Finlay Cook arrived, the church was poorly attended and it was in considerable debt. His spiritually enriching ministry, however, began to draw people, and young folks found his manner attractive. The 'Separatists' who lived around Inverness were also glad to wait upon his ministry for they found his

---

[3] Murdo MacAulay *Aspects of the Religious History of Lewis*, Stornoway, c1980, p. 76.

preaching to be the finest of the wheat, and over and above it was powerful and decisive. Sage tells us that when he began his sermon, although there appeared an awkwardness and lack of fluency in his words, yet soon "he was borne onward, not by anything in himself, but exclusively by his subject. His hearers at once participated in the heavenly influence. Their minds were both roused and arrested; every eye was directed to him, whilst the deep anxiety depicted on their countenances betokened the entrance of words, as 'words of fire' into their very inmost souls. Their former but ill-concealed apathy disappeared and was followed by an almost breathless attention. It might truly be said that, 'they who came to scoff remained to pray.'"4

He preached every Sabbath in both Gaelic and English and when one who was struck by his cosmopolitan Gaelic asked where he acquired it, his reply was, "Oh, it is a hotch-potch gathered from Arran, Lewis, Inverness, and Caithness." His stay in Inverness was too short for it to make the impact upon the town that his brother's made.

In 1835 he was called to the parish of Reay and here he remained for the rest of his days until his death in 1858 when he had reached the age of eighty years. When the Disruption took place in 1843 he signed the *Act of Separation and Deed of Demission* and became the Free Church minister of the parish. A church was built and a manse erected in 1844. The church was linked with Thurso Free Church in 1975 but today the Old Reay building lies empty and derelict.

Finlay Cook had his personal sorrows. Two of his children died in infancy but he acquiesced in his heavenly Father's will for him. Speaking to friends on one occasion, he said, "I had a little girl once, such a pretty little girl, but I made an idol of her, and just as she was beginning to walk, God took her away from me. If you have anything in this world, and make an idol of it, the Lord will take it from you, or leave it to be a curse to you." Three years after his removal to Reay he suffered further bereavement. His wife died in 1838 leaving him devastated and a grieving

---

4 Sage, *Memorabilia Domestica*, pp. 296-7.

widower for the remainder of his days. "In no way," he once said, "could I see that my wife's death was of the 'all things that work together for my good,' except the word of the Lord had said so.

As he approached the end of his life, he became more heavenly minded and longed for the salvation of the lost. Alexander Auld, the biographer of Dr John Kennedy, when he was a young minister, went to Reay to preach for his old colleague and asked him,

"What am I to say to your people?"

"Tell them they are sinners."

"What more?"

"That they need a Saviour."

"Anything more?"

"Yes, yes; that they must be born again."

He gave expression to a sense of his own unworthiness by saying,

"I am a great sinner – the greatest sinner in Caithness."

"The people of Caithness don't think so."

"No," he replied, "because there is a veil over it."

A granite obelisk was erected in his memory outside the Reay Free Church. Today it stands in the grounds of Thurso Free Church. On one side it reads, 'Erected by Congregation and Friends in memory of their revered Pastor Rev. Finlay Cook whose remains are interred in the aisles in Reay Churchyard 2 Cor. 6:3 and 10. Early called of God in Arran, his native place he laboured successively in Lanark, in Caithness, Lewis, Inverness, finally for 23 years in this Parish.' On another side of the stone these words is inscribed 'Hebrews 13, verse 7' and: 'A servant for Christ for more than fifty years. Instant in season and out of season. He was esteemed and loved throughout the north for his holy unblemished life, prudence, and faithfulness, but chiefly for the power and unction of his preaching which the Lord greatly honoured in the conversion of sinners and edifying of the saints.'

This man from Arran who was converted to God under the powerful preaching of the Rev. Neil McBride left his mark upon Inverness and the northern highlands in general. Among the many who lived and preached in those far away days the plain man from Arran is had in remembrance, and his name is still revered by those who love the old evangelical gospel.

When Finlay Cook left Inverness for Reay in 1835 the East Church was faced with the problem of finding a suitable successor. A number in the congregation set their hearts on Finlay's brother, Archibald, but another section was set on securing the Rev. David Campbell, the minister of Innerwick in Glenlyon. He was famed for the eloquence and purity of his Gaelic preaching, and by the narrowest majority he was chosen and admitted to the charge. Later he became minister of Tarbat and then of Lawers in Perthshire.

The North Church 1837 - 1893

North Church, Inverness.
Opened in 1837.

The substantial minority, however, who favoured Archibald Cook, were determined to have him and they took advantage of Dr Chalmers' Church Extension Scheme and petitioned the Inverness Presbytery for a new *"quod sacra* parish." They were successful and the North Church was built on what was then known as North Place near Friars Street. The building was a plain unadorned structure built for numbers rather than comfort and was completed and opened in 1837.

Archie Cook was admitted as first minister of the charge on 31st August 1837. The structure served the congregation for the next fifty years until it was replaced in 1893 by the present fine building on Bank Street. The old church was disposed of and has been used at different times as a store house, a sale room, and for other purposes. It has in recent years been purchased by the Elim Pentecostal Church, and refurbished by them as a place of worship. It is situated opposite the cemetery on Chapel Street and adjoins the Free Presbyterian Church buildings.

In his student days in Glasgow, Archie Cook like his brother Finlay, attended the ministry of Dr John Love of Anderston Street Church of Scotland (Glasgow) (1757-1825). Let Principal John Macleod describe John Love for us: "He was one of the most massive men of his generation,...His zeal in the cause of Foreign missions made him...one of the moving spirits of the Glasgow Missionary Society. At Anderston he had a great congregation that rallied about his ministry, and there he became the recognised centre of the Old School gospel folk of the West of Scotland. He was a man of a great mind with majestic type of thought."[5] Dr Love's *Memorials* in two volumes (1857-8), along with his other works are sought after to this day. This was the man from whom Cook learned much and sometimes the great man unburdened himself to the insignificant student. One of Cook's memories was of a Sabbath in Anderston Street Church when Dr Love was serving the communion table and suddenly his face became deathlike and a hush descended on the congregation. Mr Cook mentioned the incident to the Doctor who explained that "he had obtained such a view of the Lord in his majesty, at the head of his own table, as to be for a few moments completely overpowered." Cook learned from Dr Love the awesomeness of God, the majesty of Christ the Redeemer, and the soul-searching operations of the Holy Spirit.

After completing his studies, Archie Cook was licensed by the Presbytery of Glasgow in 1822 and the following year he was ordained and inducted missionary of the Berriedale-Bruan Mission in Caithness. Here he remained for fourteen happy years of blessing in his first charge.

If we were to go by appearance and stature of a person then this preacher would leave us unimpressed. In his book, *Ministers and Men in the Far North*, Alexander Auld describes him as a small man with a light step, a downward look, and deep-set piercing eyes that flashed like fire when he became animated.[6] Sometimes he had a dishevelled appearance. Someone

---

[5] John Macleod, *Scottish Theology*, Edinburgh, ²1946, pp. 220-1.
[6] Alexander Auld, *Ministers and Men in the Far North*, Edinburgh and Glasgow, ²1891, p. 85.

who had never seen him before and who had gone to hear him preach was greatly disappointed when he saw a slight dark minister, of shrinking manner enter the pulpit. "That cannot be Archibald Cook," he thought, as he reconciled himself to listen to the stranger. But when the service was over he realised that it must be Cook and he confessed that he had never heard a preacher like him. What Cook lacked in appearance he made up for in the spiritual qualities of his life and preaching. Although Donald Sage in his *Memorabilia* says of Cook that he had a limited range of intellectual abilities,[7] yet Principal John Macleod regarded him as a religious genius,[8] and Professor J. R. Mackay's estimate of him was that "he must have been a man of great mental vigour."[9] Sage, however, does lavish unqualified praise on him for his deep spirituality and holy zeal. He writes: "I question if there be any of the age in which we live who, in pure disinterested zeal, in holy abstractedness from the world, in vital godliness, or in exclusive devotedness to the eternal interest of the kingdom of heaven, more nearly approximates to the divinely-trained disciples of Galilee than does Archibald Cook."[10] That is praise indeed from Sage.

The Cook brothers were warmly attached to each other and the natural bond that bound them was strengthened by the bond that bound them together in the gospel. When Finlay was at Achrenny (Halkirk, Caithness) and Archibald at Berriedale it meant that the brothers laboured together in the same Presbytery for a few years. In the Presbytery there was the famous Alexander Gunn under whose ministry Watten became a veritable garden of the Lord, and sometimes he would have the assistance of the Cook brothers at his communion. John Munro of Halkirk was another famous Caithness minister who presented the gospel in a most winsome and attractive way. The young Walter Ross Taylor was beginning his memorable ministry in Thurso which was to last from 1831 until his death in 1896. Apart from the ministers there were men like Sandy Gair,

---

7 Sage, *Memorabilia Domestica*, p. 400.
8 John Macleod, *By-paths of Highland Church History*, Edinburgh, 1965, p. 105.
9 See Mackay, *Sermons in Gaelic and English by Rev. A. Cook*, p. xviii.
10 Sage, *Memorabilia Domestica*, pp. 400-1.

Joseph Mackay, and David Steven, along with a host of soundly converted men and women who graced the county. Today, as in other places, exercised Christians can only lament the spiritual barrenness that has overtaken districts that once rejoiced in the Lord, and like the prophet lament, "How is the gold become dim! How is the most fine gold changed." (Lamentations 4:1).

In this most northerly part of Scotland, Archie Cook began his ministry and seized the opportunities that were presented to him. Eight miles away was the busy fishing town of Wick with many herring boats arriving at the harbour with their catches. These boats were manned by fishermen from the west as well as from Aberdeenshire and as far south as Eyemouth. They needed to hear the gospel as did those on shore who cleaned the fish. In Cook's reckoning this was a mission field and week by week he made his way to Wick to preach especially to the Gaelic speaking fishermen from the west. When he left Caithness, the work was so well established that it was carried on by Sandy Gair for as long as he was in the vicinity. Afterwards the Free Church saw to it that those who "go down to the sea in ships, that do business in great waters" (Psalm 107:23) were provided for spiritually.

The Berriedale-Bruan mission at that time contained Latheron, and Cook strenuously set about disseminating the gospel among the people in every way possible. Apart from preaching regularly every Lord's Day, he catechized throughout the winter months. In these diets, as they were called, of catechizing, there would gather a number of families in a home and by use of the *Shorter Catechism* and the Bible each would be asked questions based upon biblical truth. The aim was not to see who had the best memory in repeating answers, but to discover whether the questions and answers were understood in the experience of the person catechized. These meetings were extremely profitable and accomplished what could never be accomplished by a mere social visit.

In the days of his Daviot ministry he catechized throughout the winter until May. Weather permitting four diets were held each week and each diet usually lasted for two or three hours, and in Daviot, because of the numbers attending such gatherings would be held in a barn. In a letter to his nephew in Glasgow written at the end of 1849 he writes, "Great numbers attend, some come from a distance of eight miles to the night diets; at times to the number of four or five hundred are present; sometimes great impressions appear among the people, but the Lord above knows the fruit. Though I find it heavy, it is the happiest part of my time in the whole year."[11]

At these meetings he would deal patiently and tenderly with a person who required a gentle touch, while on the other hand he could be severe if that was required. "What," he asked someone, "was the highest mountain you ever climbed?" and he went on to answer his question, "As for myself the highest mountain I ever met was to believe that there was a God." On another occasion he put it to the people, "You who borrow your religion from books and other Christians, on the great day of the Lord, when every book will get its own, and every Christian will get his own, what will be left with you? Another time he remarked, "There will be many an enlightened head at the left hand but no broken heart." A word of warning was addressed to parents, "Children may often say to their parents, – 'Father, your prayers in the family are not very good; but if your life was half as good, we would be the better of you.'"

How much he read of Puritan Literature, or of the old Scottish Divines, we cannot say, but without question he was familiar with the Bible and with the Reformed teachings outlined in the *Confession of Faith*. In comparing him with the Rev. Alexander Gunn of Watten, Auld says, "Mr Gunn, although richly experimental, was...pre-eminently doctrinal, both in respect of law and gospel – in law, largely exhibiting man's conditions, character, and prospects under a broken covenant; in gospel, unfolding the person, work and offices of the Redeemer. Mr. Cook again, though richly doctrinal, was pre-eminent in his analysis of the human heart – regenerate and unregenerate. In this department he had almost unrivalled power...It was his delineation of graceless human nature...that

---

[11] *Sidelights on Two Notable Ministries*, Inverness, 1970, p. 115.

roused against him so often and so bitterly the resentment of the 'seed of the serpent,' and made them strive to discover in his speech and manner matter of ridicule."[12] Cook's ministry was greatly prized by many of the Lord's people to such an extent that they were in danger of idolising the man, and those who followed him wherever he preached were dubbed 'The Cookites.'

After his settlement in Bruan he married Miss Catherine Mackay of Wick. They had a family of two sons and six daughters; one of the daughters married her cousin, Alexander Cook, the son of Finlay Cook, who, as we have already said, was Free Church minister of Stratherrick, and who died in 1862 at the early age of thirty-seven. Archie's fourteen years in Bruan were happy and spiritually profitable, when, as he used to say, the Aarons and the Hurs held up his arms in Caithness.

The new Inverness North Church was supported by some of the finest Christian people in the town and even a number of the 'Separatists' in the area approved of the new minister to the extent that they gave him their support. During the seven years he was in Inverness the congregation grew steadily and rejoiced in the gospel as it was proclaimed by him. His brother Finlay was able to write of that period, "My brother Archibald, is doing very well in Inverness. He is well liked by the people. I was three nights with him last winter, on my way home from Edinburgh. He is really an excellent man; there are few in this generation like him, I never saw a man that keeps so near to the Lord as he does. I am not worth a straw beside him; he is continually praying, reading, or meditating, when he is not engaged in public. Though you were a year with him you would not hear a vain word out of his mouth." His own estimate of himself, however, was very different. Writing to a friend at this time, he says, "My own barrenness and distance from God, the want of spiritual mindedness, and the fear of becoming a barren tree in the church, these often make my life a burden, and I often wish that I never appeared in public, or that I had been born dumb."

---

[12] Auld, *Ministers and Men in the Far North*, pp. 78-9.

In Inverness he was not only preacher to a devoted and attached congregation but he became a power of moral good to the town. His fearlessness in expressing his displeasure at what he considered unseemly behaviour brought him into conflict with the disreputable functions known as 'Penny Weddings' which were then common. These weddings were held in public houses where all were made welcome so long as they paid the fiddler and purchased his drink, but the moral tone of such festivities was questionable to say the least. His experience of the dancing school in Arran made him averse to what Christians call "promiscuous dancing," and he deplored the excessive use of alcohol. By protest and by actively opposing 'Penny Weddings' he managed to bring the practice to an end. Today he might be dismissed by many as being too restrictive and old fashioned but on the dancing question, Archie Cook stands in the company of Professor John Duncan, Professor Robert L. Dabney, Isobel Kuhn and many others.

In their Caithness days the Cook brothers developed a warm friendship with Joseph Mackay and other 'Separatists.' It would appear that when Archibald Cook was minister of the North Church, Joseph Mackay who was then living at Raigbeg Schoolhouse in Strathdearn, attended the North Church and was regarded as the congregation's catechist. At any rate Principal Macleod says that "in the early accounts of the congregation there is an entry of a special collection for Joseph Mackay, catechist."[13] But however close the friendship between Cook and Mackay an estrangement developed. Mackay and his fellow 'Separatists' opposed Church patronage and its abuses but they did not approve of the breaking up of the Established Church and they distanced themselves from the Disruption. On the other hand, the Cook brothers sided with the evangelical party and welcomed the Disruption and became ardent Free Churchmen.

In his opposition to Archie Cook, Joseph Mackay raised points in what he regarded as defects in the minister's preaching. One defect had to

---

[13] Macleod, *By-paths of Highland Church History*, p. 106.

19

do with the order of the Divine decree. One group in Reformed circles are called Supralapsarians. They place God's predestination of the elect first and then his permissive decree to allow "the Fall" next. The other group called Infralapsarians place God's permissive decree to allow "The Fall" first, and then his Predestination of the Elect next. Professor Finlayson says: "Our Confessional Standards, while not condemning Supralapsarianism, embody the Infralapsarian position." Principal Macleod says that Cook was "not a Hyper-Calvinist, but he was a Supralapsarian; and he did not hide his light."[14] Another point that Joseph Mackay made was that Cook was a Traducian. This has to do with the origin of the soul. There are those called 'Creationists' who believe that each individual soul is created by God and owes nothing of its origin to parents. This does raise the difficulty that if the soul is individually created by God it must be innocent, and if so, then at what stage does it become sinful in the womb? Others, called 'Traducians', believe that the soul along with the body comes from the parents. Two of the greatest American theologians of the 19th century differed on this point. Charles Hodge was a creationist, while William G. T. Shedd was a traducian. In Reformed circles the creationist view is the acceptable one. Archie Cook, however, was pronounced traducian, while Joseph Mackay took the ordinary position of orthodox Reformed Doctrine. In the dispute Principal John Macleod describes Archibald Cook as "dogmatic, militant, and aggressive."[15] Sage confirms this trait in Cook's character where he says, "If anyone departs a hair's-breadth from his own precise view of Scriptural doctrine or religious experience, he stands in doubt of him."[16]

These disputes show how deeply people thought in the realms of theology, how sappy the preaching must have been, and how the hearers were people of keen perception and discernment. When Joseph Mackay was gravely ill, Archie Cook visited him and the men were reconciled.

---

[14] As above, p. 105
[15] As above.
[16] Sage, *Memorabilia Domestica*, p. 400.

Mackay died at Raigbeg Schoolhouse in 1848 and is buried in the Chapel Yard, Inverness.

When Cook arrived in Inverness in 1837 the "Ten Years Conflict" in the Church of Scotland was underway when everything legally possible was done to have the Patronage Act (1711) rescinded. All efforts failed with the inevitable Disruption of the Church of Scotland and the emergence of the Free Church of Scotland in 1843. The Cook brothers had made up their minds about which side to take and they with many others signed the *Act of Separation and Deed of Demission* whereby they became ministers of the Free Church. Archibald Cook's entire congregation sided with him and entered the Free Church. Since the building had been put up at the people's expense the congregation was not dispossessed of its property as other congregations were. Cook's ministry in the town was soon to end.

In the 1830s the minister of the Parish Church of Daviot was James MacPhail son of the well-known Hector MacPhail who taught the highland kitchen maid to pray, "Lord shew me myself" and later to pray, "Lord shew me Thyself," which was the means used in her conversion. When James MacPhail died in 1839, the patron attempted to set over the congregation a man who was quite unacceptable to the people and the Daviot case eventually had to come before the courts of the church. In the struggle Archibald Cook expressed his sympathy with the Daviot people and they in turn regarded him highly and as one who would make a suitable pastor for them. Consequently, after the Disruption and in the summer of 1843 the way was now open for the Daviot people to call the minister of their own choice, namely Archibald Cook. The North Church, however, took steps to thwart this move. A statement was prepared and signed by more than nine hundred persons and presented to Inverness Presbytery not to sanction Mr Cook's removal from the town. The statement in itself was an eloquent tribute to Mr Cook and showed the deep affection in which he was held by his people. It also stated that if Mr. Cook was released from his charge it would be a devastating loss to the Free North congregation. When the matter came before Presbytery, Cook realizing the warmth of his people's attachment to him placed himself in the hands of his brethren who declined to place the call in his hands.

The following year the Daviot congregation approached him a second time and feeling that town life was prejudicial to his health, he allowed them to proceed in the matter. The North congregation indicated that if Mr Cook felt it to be his duty to go to Daviot then they would not oppose the call. Archibald Cook was inducted to Daviot on 1st August, 1844. The call addressed to Rev. John MacQueen, Mr Cook's successor in 1866 contains 640 names, and when you add to that the many young people under the age of 18 who were not allowed to sign, it gives an indication of the strength of the Daviot congregation in the days of Archibald Cook's ministry. Here he laboured among people who were warmly attached to him, and there were many who came considerable distances to listen to the man from Arran who exposed the depravity of the human heart and who pointed to Christ Jesus the only sure remedy.

As he advanced in years life became lonely for him through bereavements. In 1851 his wife died a comparatively young woman, and referring to her passing he wrote, "She has left us mourning after her…I am now a poor lonely person, and will be so all my days." His brother, Finlay, died in 1858. His son-in-law and nephew, the Rev. Alex Cook, Stratherrick died in 1862. In 1863 his strong frame began to give way and after repeated strokes which left him paralysed, he died in 1865. He is buried in Dunlichity Churchyard among many of his beloved flock and an impressive stone marks his resting place.

In the vestibule of the present Free North building on Bank Street, Inverness, there is an inscribed tablet which reads,

> After his death, David Steven, one of the eminent men of Caithness wrote to a friend, "That bright star in our Church has set, — The Rev. Archibald Cook, — one of deeper acquaintance with Divine things than has appeared for many a day."

Such was the man who became the first minister of the Free North Church in Inverness.

CHAPTER 2

GEORGE MACKAY

ARCHIBALD COOK'S TRANSLATION to the new Daviot Free Church in 1844 initiated the quest to find a successor to replace him in Inverness. The choice was George Mackay, minister of Clyne Free Church in the Presbytery of Dornoch.

George Mackay was born at Strath Halladale in 1796 in the parish of Reay. Reay parish was then partly in Sutherland and partly in Caithness; today it is in Caithness. In the early 18th century, Reay, like many parts of the north of Scotland, languished in pagan darkness; the people were primitive and lacking in refinement. But into that situation came a young minister whose pioneering methods in spreading the gospel were to say the least quite unorthodox. He was Alexander Pope, who, according to Sage, was "an accomplished classical scholar, an intelligent antiquary, and was intimately conversant with science."[17] He was related to the famous English poet Alexander Pope whose classical poems 'The Rape of the Lock,' 'The Dunciad,' 'The Iliad,' 'The Odyssey,' and others have made his name famous in English Literature. His sayings, "A little learning is a dangerous thing!" and "To err is human: to forgive, divine," are still quoted today.

---

[17] Sage, *Memorabilia Domestica*, p. 43.

The Rev. Donald Beaton in his informative volume, *Some Noted Ministers of the Northern Highlands*, tells us that when he was a young man Pope, the minister, went to London to see his celebrated namesake. "Their meeting to begin with was cold and stiff but after being in contact with the strong, well-furnished intellect of his Scottish namesake, the poet relaxed and the men had mutual respect for each other."[18] The young minister was presented with a signed copy of a recent publication of the poet's poems.

Alexander Pope, the minister whose ancestors belonged to the Anglican Church, had, by conviction, become a Presbyterian. After completing his studies for the ministry, he was ordained and inducted to the charge of Reay in 1734. The Rev. Donald Beaton describes the people of Reay at that time as, "not only ignorant, but coarse in their manners, and vicious in their dispositions."[19] There was about them a degree of savagery which they expressed in their profane behaviour, their uninhibited language, and their contempt and disregard of the Lord's Day. They were more at home in the tavern than in the church. The young minister was undaunted. Before him lay a promising field and he set about the task of cultivating it by proclaiming the authority and majesty of God's Law, and the redeeming grace of God in the gospel of Christ. Pope was a pious man of tireless energy and extraordinary strength which he used in the service of his master. The times called for unusual methods to be employed in his work and these he used. He carried about with him a small cudgel called "the bailey" which he never hesitated to wield with force if a situation required it, and many a drunkard or profane person had cause to nurse a sore head after being dealt with by the minister. In spite of his rough edge and unorthodox methods, Pope was honoured in seeing a time of blessing coming to the parish of Reay. As he advanced in age he mellowed and latterly he became disabled and had to be carried to his

---

[18] Donald Beaton, *Some Noted Ministers of the Northern Highlands*, Inverness, 1929, p. 54.
[19] As above, p. 55.

church in a litter. He died mourned and lamented by an attached flock. He is buried in Reay cemetery.

Rev. David Mackay, his successor, was an entirely different type of person. He was a quiet, peaceable man who suffered from nervous breakdowns. His sanctified life, however, was an influence in itself and made an impact upon the community. Another whose influence was for the everlasting benefit of the Reay people was that of James Macdonald, the catechist. He was the father of the famous minister, John Macdonald, otherwise known as 'The Apostle of the North.' Although James Macdonald did not have the status of a minister of the gospel, yet he was a highly esteemed Christian layman whom the people respected and to whom they turned with their spiritual problems. He was a man of faith and godliness who rendered valuable service to the cause of Christ in the remote part of Scotland where he lived.

These were the spiritual influences that prevailed in the Reay country towards the end of the eighteenth century, when spiritual blight in the north began to lift. It could then be said of these remote areas as it could be of other parts of Scotland, "...lo, the winter is past, the rain is over and gone; The flowers appear on the earth; the time of the singing of birds is come, and the voice of the turtle[-dove] is heard in our land" (Song of Solomon 2:11-12).

As the nineteenth century approached, a new day of promise was breaking, and on a Sabbath at the end of June, 1796, George Mackay was born. We know very little of his background. His parents were God-fearing, and whether he was their only child we cannot now say. Certain it is that they impressed upon their son the truths of God's Word and he was the subject of their prayers. His daughter tells us that he inherited from his father, "his great judgment and intellect; and from his mother the warm-hearted, generous nature, and the tact and grace of manner which so distinguished him." All that we can now say of his early days is that he received a liberal education at the local parish school which prepared him for entrance to Aberdeen University. He enrolled at King's College and completed the prescribed course for the ministry. We do not know when he was converted, but that he loved the Saviour and served him faithfully throughout a long and distinguished ministry is beyond question.

As a young man he made an indelible impression upon people. He was tall and handsome and there was an air of superiority about him. His trustworthiness and integrity impressed parents of other boys who were students, so that they urged him to keep a watchful and kindly eye on their sons, for they knew that he would only influence them for good. In his assessment of Mackay, the Rev. Norman C. Macfarlane in his book, *Apostles of the North* has this to say about him: "he was straight as a die, and carefully picked his steps amid life's puddles. [Parents] knew their boys would be all right under his care. This kind of respect which he inspired in his early life, he continued to inspire to the very end. Everywhere George Mackay was looked up to."[20] During vacation time he procured employment as teacher of the parish school in Loth in Sutherland, and this helped to finance him with his studies in Aberdeen. Being a teacher before becoming a minister was both an advantage and a disadvantage to him. The advantage was that in imparting knowledge he had learned to put things simply, clearly, and orderly. The disadvantage was that he tended to treat his congregation as if they were children in a classroom.

In 1827 he was licensed to preach by the Presbytery of Dornoch, and soon afterwards he was appointed assistant to the Rev. Dr Angus Mackintosh of Tain. Dr Mackintosh was an outstanding preacher in Easter Ross who proclaimed the majesty of God's Law, who showed forth the grandeur and purity of the holiness of God, who revealed the awfulness of the human heart in its depraved sinfulness, and who offered the finished work of Christ as the only remedy for the sinner. Angus Mackintosh was a burning and shining light in his day and there was fervour, zeal, and power in his pulpit work. He was used mightily in gathering many into the kingdom of Christ the Saviour. His son, who befriended George Mackay, was the saintly and scholarly Dr Charles Calder Mackintosh who succeeded his father as minister of Tain and who

---

[20] Norman C. Macfarlane, *Apostles of the North*, Stornoway, no date, p. 90.

later became minister of Dunoon Free Church. A memorial volume of the life and ministry of Charles Calder Mackintosh was produced and edited by the Rev. William Taylor of Stirling and printed in 1870. The volume shows Charles Mackintosh to have been a truly outstanding man. George Mackay lived and laboured in Tain until his ordination and induction to Clyne Parish Church in 1828, and he ever afterwards acknowledged the benefit he derived from the influence of both father and son in the Tain manse.

In 1828 Mackay was presented to the parish of Clyne, a presentation which he accepted because it was accompanied by a unanimous call. The fifteen years that he stayed in the vicinity of Brora were years of happiness and blessing. Not far away was Dunrobin Castle, the residence of the Duke of Sutherland, and with the coming and going of high society to the castle the stylish fashions of the south began to influence the north. We are told, for example, that the younger women dressed well, wore straw bonnets, and braided their hair. George Mackay did not discourage this: he was a man of refinement and taste who exercised a leavening influence over the manners of the people, and he was impeccable in his own dress. At the same time he was a man of God, a rousing preacher whose clarity of thought and solid statements of Divine truth profoundly affected his hearers and brought conviction to their minds. He became intimately acquainted with the Sutherland household and was a favourite guest at their table. His intelligence and frankness endeared him to many of the illustrious visitors to the castle among whom were Lord Palmerston and Lord Brougham, and the old Duchess of Sutherland esteemed her minister highly. In the case of a lesser man this attention and esteem from such a noble source might have proved too much, and made him suppress his personal convictions in order to please the superior. Mackay, however, was made of better stuff.

The 1830s were critical years for the Church. The debates in General Assembly about non-intrusion (anti-patronage), as it was called, and the doctrine of the Headship of Christ over his church became more vigorous with the passing of the years. Attitudes between moderates and evangelicals hardened and it was obvious that both sides were coming to the parting of the ways. The Disruption of the church was approaching. Ministers, office-bearers, and people, had to decide whether to remain in an establishment which did not give Christ his place as Head, or to quit the establishment for a church that would allow Christ to be Head over His own house. George Mackay had made up his mind irrespective of the cost to himself, and he let it be known where his sympathies lay. He prepared his people so that they understood the issues that were involved, and their confidence in their young minister was such that when the separation from the state church came most of them followed him without any hesitation.

The attitude of the Sutherland household towards the minister changed dramatically. There was a cooling of affection towards him and no longer was he invited to be a guest at their table. But George Mackay never wavered in his adherence to Free Church principles. Alexander Macrae in his biography of Dr Aird sums up Mackay's character in these words. "The Rev. George Mackay, Clyne, was, perhaps, the most striking personality in the Presbytery. He had already made for himself a great name as a fearless and faithful preacher, and as an uncompromising supporter of the Church's freedom and spiritual independence. Up till the Disruption, he had, in the Duchess of Sutherland, a warm admirer and friend. When she was in residence at the Castle he was often invited there. After that there was a coldness, but the common people heard him gladly, and feared him greatly, and he was so much engrossed in his work that he thought but little of the loss of her friendship."[21]

He was appointed a member of the historic General Assembly of 1843 but because of an accident in which he sustained a compound fracture of an arm he was unable to attend the Assembly. He did, however, sign the *Act of Separation and Deed of Demission* and thereby ceased being a minister of the Established Church and became a minister of the Free Church of Scotland. He now had to leave the comfortable parish manse, relinquish

---

[21] Alexander Macrae, *Life of Gustavus Aird*, Inverness, 1908, p. 121.

its glebe, and forfeit his stipend. This could not have been easy as he had the responsibility for supporting a wife and family. A small cottage was placed at his disposal where he and his family found shelter and a barn was used as a place of worship. These were trying times when he was homeless, churchless, and without income. But, "There is no man that hath left house, or brethren, or sisters, or father, or mother, or wife, or children, or lands, for my sake, and the gospel's, but he shall receive an hundredfold no in this time, houses, and brethren, and sisters, and mothers, and children, and lands, with persecutions; and in the world to come eternal life" (Mark 10:29-30).

The period between leaving the Established Church and the formation of the new Free Church was a time when many problems had to be faced. Everything that could be done to thwart the people from supporting the new Church was done. Landlords who were not in sympathy with the Free Church offered whatever resistance they could, and wherever possible prevented the sale of sites to the new Church. Although George Mackay suffered from a broken arm and his health was undermined by the strain of the times, yet he pursued vigorously his search for a site and manse with zeal, energy, and enthusiasm. On 27th May, 1843, he wrote the following urgent letter to an eminent layman, Mr. Patrick Tennant of Edinburgh:

> My dear Sir,
>
> I beg leave to request of you, as a member of Assembly, to intimate my adherence to the protest given in by my brethren, and my readiness, by the grace of God, to share in the consequences. My serious accident, and the present state of my health render it utterly impossible for me to be in Edinburgh on the present momentous occasion.
>
> I enclose a copy of a deed which I have in my hands, of a lot of land in the village of Brora, which I earnestly request you to lay before the Provisional Committee. It is of the very utmost importance that the matter be attended to without one moment's delay: otherwise the chance will be that the property will be bought up, and that the only site which can be got on any terms, so far as I can learn, will be taken from us.

This station is surrounded by three parishes where there are three Moderate ministers, and I am not aware that a single piece of ground can be got in any of them for erecting a place of worship, unless in the village of Helmsdale. From Brora there is access to any of them on a Sabbath morning, and the people adhering to the Free Church could attend in this parish as they often do, even should they not have the ordinances of religion administered regularly among themselves.

Let me urge upon you the absolute necessity of attending punctually with this document. Everything here depends upon whether or not we can procure the site, for I can scarcely move the people on till they see before them the prospect of a place of worship, and you have no conception of the efforts that are being made to keep them back from joining us, and the extraordinary influence those in authority have over them.

I am, my dear sir, Yours sincerely,

George Mackay.

Mr. Mackay was successful, the site was secured and the difficulties which had been put in the way of the formation of a new Brora Free Church were set aside. But Mackay was not to remain in Clyne for much longer. The Free North congregation which had become vacant in 1844 had set their sights on this man who was now in his prime, and who had proved himself a strong leader of men. When he intimated that he was leaving Sutherland a worthy Clyne elder approached him and asked:

"Why? Are we not kind enough to you Mr. Mackay?"

"Do you see that pool in the river, Donald? What would you do if you could find no fish there?"

"Oh, I would move on to the next pool," said Donald.

"Well," replied Mackay, "that is exactly what I am doing in moving on to Inverness."

The call from the North Church was unanimous and was signed by 1,235 persons and in June, 1845, he was inducted to the charge, and here for the next forty-one years he laboured in Inverness. Throughout these years the congregation necessarily changed as one generation succeeded another, but the numbers attending never diminished but rather increased.

When George Mackay arrived in Inverness the town was astir with religious excitement caused by the Disruption. The Disruption was no mere splinter group, rather a considerable number of ministers, 481 (plus 27 overseas missionaries) to be precise, quit the Established Church, signed the *Act of Separation and Deed of Demission*, and formed themselves into the Church of Scotland Free. In the majority of cases the congregations of those ministers almost to a man followed their ministers, and substantial majorities in other congregations where the ministers remained in the Establishment, threw in their lot with the Free Church.

Rev. George Mackay

There were reasons for the Disruption and its success. First, there was a vital principle at stake which was the Headship of Christ over his Church. That principle is at the core of Scottish Presbyterianism. The Stuart kings endeavoured to suppress it and the Church's freedom in favour of their belief in 'The Divine Right of Kings.' But our Scottish ancestors refused to allow interference by the Monarch or the State in the affairs of Christ's Church, and irrespective of cost to themselves stoutly maintained the freedom of the Kirk in her own province. The Disruption was about freedom. Patrons or Governments had no right whatever to impose upon the Church what was not ordained by God. Secondly, the Disruption happened at a time when Scotland was in the throes of a great movement of the Spirit of God. Congregations and individuals were being affected in a remarkable way in places like Kilsyth, Dundee, Ferintosh, Speyside, Badenoch, and other parts of Scotland. The lifeless moderatism that had prevailed for so long in the old Kirk was swept aside by an

31

evangelical force that had been unknown for decades. The Church of Christ was on the march and souls were being brought into the Kingdom of God in great numbers, so that when separation from lifeless orthodoxy was called for, the call was responded to without hesitation. Another reason for the success of the Disruption was that the political climate in Scotland was changing, and the middle classes were able to express opposition to unscrupulous landlords who for long had exploited them in Kirk and State.

The Disruption, even as a protest vote, was popular, and the early successes of the new Church were phenomenal. Her energy, vision, and zeal, were displayed in her staggering programme of advancing the Kingdom of God on earth. A plan for financing the work of the Church was initiated by Dr Chalmers called 'The Sustentation Fund,' and the idea behind the fund remains to this day the bedrock of the Church's income. It was a matter of giving to the cause of God,, as He has prospered you, and in our day we judge that to mean placing at the Lord's disposal a tenth of what you earn. The first twenty years of the new church's existence were outstanding, and some have suggested that in terms of devotion to our Lord and purity of practice nothing has been seen like it since the days of the Apostles.

In Inverness, when Mackay arrived, there was a mood of expectancy. Not only was the North Church caught up in the excitement of the times, but so too was the East Church which also had joined the Free Church under its minister, the Rev. David Sutherland. The Free Church began to grow in the town. A number of adherents formed themselves into a congregation and called themselves 'The English Free Church' later renamed 'The Free High Church.' They built on the riverside in 1852 near where the present North building stands. In 1900 they joined the United Free Church and in 1929 the Church of Scotland. They are now called St. Columba Church. Another Free Church called the West Free Church was built on that side of the river in 1863. This Church is now Trinity Church of Scotland. Queen Street Church, which was originally a United Presbyterian Church, was admitted to the Free Church in 1873. It also became a Church of Scotland in 1929. The building now belongs to Chisholm's the Undertaker. Later in the century the Crown Free Church was built in 1898. It, too, joined the United Free Church in 1900 and the Church of Scotland in 1929.

The North Church was the principal Gaelic church in the town and three services were conducted each Lord's Day. The morning one was wholly in Gaelic, and the afternoon and evening services were generally in English. In those days, there were really two congregations in the North Church: one Gaelic and the other English. Mackay was a bilingual preacher and as it was said of Dr Kennedy, so it could be said of him, that when he preached in Gaelic it was as though he knew little English, and when he preached in English one could hardly believe that he knew any Gaelic. He had a commanding presence, a fine clear sonorous voice, and an impressive and earnest pulpit style. His sermon preparation was meticulous and Saturday was spent in his study except for a short break out of doors in his beautifully laid out garden. Rev. Norman C. Macfarlane writes, "His habits were admirable. On the principle that it is the early bird that gets the rations, he rose with the beam of the day. In all his engagements he was as exact as a timetable. He studied carefully and preached thrice every Sabbath day. He had time to cultivate his own family notwithstanding the claims of the largest congregation in Inverness."[22]

The manse that was procured for Mr Mackay was a substantial building on Church Street situated at the top of Church Lane. It is now a hotel, called the MacDougall Clansman Hotel. When a manse, it had a large garden behind the house which stretched down to the riverside. The garden is now the site upon which the present Free North Church building stands. In a sketch by way of a tribute to the memory of her father, Mackay's youngest daughter Violette describes the manse garden in a most picturesque and attractive manner. She writes: "As one entered the gate from the dingy street, it was a most pleasing surprise to see the smooth green lawn with its little plots and borders of gaily coloured and varied

---

[22] Macfarlane, *Apostles of the North*, p. 92.

hothouse plants. There was a chestnut tree and yellow laburnum. There was pink hawthorn, and the scent of lilac filled the air with its fragrance. Beyond the lawn were the fruit and flower gardens, and right at the foot were three tall stately trees. With only the garden wall and roadway between, the beautiful and majestic river flowed, where on summer days the sunbeams danced and shone like so many diamonds, but lovelier still, to my mind, was the reflection of the moon lighting up the dark water."[23] In this garden George Mackay relaxed in favourable weather, and here he found peace and tranquillity, and here, as his daughter tells us, he would walk up and down the gravel path followed by the large household cat of which he was very fond.

We have no means of knowing what his preaching was like for nothing has survived from his ministry by way of printed sermons. He gave strict instructions to his family that nothing he had ever written was to be published after his death and that trust was kept. Violette writes: "After my mother was gone I found among her private papers two sermons of his, which she had evidently kept for occasional perusal. Not knowing into whose hands at some future time they might fall, with great reluctance I consigned them to the flames; and as I watched the last ashes smouldering, felt a melancholy satisfaction in thinking that I had fulfilled the trust left to me."[24]

Mr Mackay was twice married. In 1831 he married Louisa Reid; and after her passing he married Catherine Fraser in 1847. Apart from Violette we do not know what other family he had. The only materials to hand which give information about Dr Mackay are the booklet by his daughter, and a sketch written by Rev. Norman C. Macfarlane of Juniper Green, Edinburgh, and included in his book *The Apostles of the North*. There is a fine tribute to the man which appeared in a little book which was printed many years ago by the *Inverness Courier* called 'Biographies of Highland

---

[23] Violette Mackay, *George Mackay — A Sketch*, pp. 26-27.
[24] As above, p. 12.

Clergymen.' It is primarily from these sources as well as some others that we glean the kind of person George Mackay was.

Along with an impressive appearance he had a strong personality and was never afraid to voice his opinions. Throughout the churches in the town he was known as, 'The Pope of the North.' We give some examples of his independence and of how outspoken he could be. It is usually unwise for a minister to urge people to vote for one party more than another, but on one occasion Mackay did so and urged that those who had the vote should cast it in favour of the Conservative candidate at the forthcoming Parliamentary election. It caused disquiet and gave offence to some, so much so, that they left his congregation and went to the East Church. Mackay was unrepentant and dismissed those who left with the withering comment, "We have fanners in the North Church that blow all our chaff to the East Church." Having made up his mind about a political issue he declared his opinion and there the matter ended.

A story has circulated involving Mackay's name and it is very much in Mackay's style. There was an elder in a neighbouring congregation with whom the Doctor had a dispute. He came to a Friday Gaelic Fellowship Meeting in the North Church. In order to pour oil on troubled waters the elder was invited to give out the question. He chose 1 Kings chapter 13, verse 13, "Saddle me the ass," and asked for true Christian marks to be given. Perhaps he thought that as such an animal is hard to break in and requires firm handling so it is with the Lord's people. Mackay thought it frivolous and his reaction was typical, "You fetch me the saddle, I've got the ass."

His fearlessness not only gained for him the appellation 'The Pope of the North,' but also 'The lion of the North.' One day when reading the pulpit intimations there was one whose import had escaped his notice and which had to do with a woman preaching in a public building in the town. He stopped, drew himself up, and speaking with all the authority at his command said, "A woman preaching! That reminds me of what happened when I was a boy. I ran into the house one day and cried out, 'mother, mother, there's a hen in the yard trying to crow.' 'Draw its neck, my boy,

35

draw its neck, and do it quick.'"[25] One wonders what the old firebrand would say of the present situation when there are women not only in the eldership of some Presbyterian Churches, but women in the ministry of the church itself!

In Presbytery too, he said what he thought. When the Free Church in the latter part of the 19th century began to waver, he stood firm. On one occasion he and Dr James Black of the Free High Church had an altercation. Black was his junior and a jovial Irishman who was frank and outspoken and had a large bare shining face. In the dispute Mackay responded, "Dare you contradict me, you beardless boy!"[26] Another minister who dared was the Rev. Duncan Calvin of the Free West Church. The two men were frequently in dispute. Because of this the Free North became uneasy and the elders decided to make a presentation to their worthy minister. They arrived at the manse and assured him of their appreciation of him as a preacher of the gospel, and as their minister. They feared controversy and hoped he would not tarnish his reputation. He immediately stopped them, there and then, and firmly told them, "I'll not take one penny of your money. It is meant to put a chain on my tongue."[27] Mackay was not the kind of man who would be bribed.

Any impression that he was a difficult and contentious person would be a slur on the man. Straight as a die and an upright minister he certainly was, but he was also a caring pastor whose hospitality and generosity knew no bounds. He loved young people and would sometimes greet them with a pat on the head or slip a copper coin into their hands. He showed a keen interest in the young people of his own congregation and watched their progress through life, as someone has put it, "as a gardener watches the tender plants which have grown under his care." Many of them he had baptised in their infancy and he observed their progress to manhood and womanhood and he would enter into their joy on their wedding day. The old church building had no hall where the young folks could gather of an

---

[25] Macfarlane, *Apostles of the North*, p. 92.
[26] As above.
[27] As above, p. 93.

evening but that did not deter him from bringing them together at the manse and in inviting them on summer evenings to play croquet on the lawn where he would join them in their pastime. Sadly, there were those of them whose days on earth were shortened, when in the mysterious Providence of God the grim reaper, who comes to us all sooner or later would pass their way. "There is a reaper and his name is death, and with his sickle keen, he reaps among the bearded grains and the flowers that grow between."

For him, as for any minister, it was a sore task visiting young people in the closing stages of their lives, and yet it gave him great comfort when he found them full of Christian faith and "looking for that city which hath foundations whose builder and whose maker is God." (Hebrews 11:10).

Seldom did he preach without earnestly appealing to the young of the congregation to "Remember their Creator in the days of their youth ere the evil days would come when they would find no pleasure in them" (see Ecclesiastes 12:1). He would lovingly urge them to seek salvation in Christ. They esteemed him highly, so much so that on one occasion they did an extraordinary thing. In 1860 they presented him with a purse of sovereigns along with a silver salver and tea service to show their esteem and appreciation of him as their minister.

Many were entertained in Mr and Mrs Mackay's hospitable manse. On the one hand it might be a group of ladies for afternoon tea, or on the other ministers who in the course of business had come to see him. His friendship extended to all classes irrespective of denominational persuasion. He loved music and having a melodious tenor voice he enjoyed listening to and singing the beautiful songs of Scotland.

As a pastor he visited his large congregation as often as possible and where there were problems he either gave advice or administered rebuke as required. An example has been recorded by his daughter of a tradesman and his wife who bitterly disagreed with each other. The husband was addicted to intemperate habits and his wife had a sharp temper. Matters came to a head and the minister's intervention was called for. When he visited them unexpectedly their conscience troubled them and his stern expression warned them of his displeasure at their behaviour. He rebuked the man for his sin and the woman for the wickedness of her tongue and temper which drove the man to intemperance. After admonishing them and praying with and for them, he took his leave. From then on, they lived changed lives and were blessed with prosperity, and became respected citizens in the town.

When he went on his visiting rounds, he took with him five pounds of change which was a considerable sum in those days. If he found a poor workman ill, he would slip a half sovereign into his wife's hand, and one here and another there would be the beneficiary of his bounty. His tender heart was revealed when frequently he would pay a poor widow's rent, or he would help financially a struggling student on his way to college. They never forgot his kindness.

There were two notable events in George Mackay's life which occurred in 1878 when he was 80 years old and which deserve to be mentioned. The first was the distinction of being awarded the honorary degree of Doctor of Divinity by his *Alma Mater*, – the University of Aberdeen.

The second was the celebration of his jubilee in the ministry which was arranged by the Free North congregation and held on Monday 15th November, 1878, in the Music Hall. The chairman for the occasion was Dr John Kennedy of Dingwall Free Church and the audience consisted of clergymen from within and outwith the Free Church, local officials and dignitaries from the town, Free North people as well as other folks.

Because of the lateness of the year some of Mackay's closest friends could not be present but they sent their apologies along with congratulatory remarks. In the fulsome account given in the *Inverness Advertiser* such names appear, Principal David Brown of the Free Church College, Aberdeen (one of Mackay's fellow students), Dr James Begg, Dr Alexander Moody Stuart, and a list of Free Church ministers from different parts of Scotland.

After these apologies, Dr Kennedy, the Chairman, then addressed the gathering and in his concluding remarks said: "I cannot hope that our service on earth can be long continued. Our days are well-nigh run out. But little more toil, but little more waiting for the Master's coming remains for us. And while I cannot but anticipate for him the prospect, I will not disclaim the hope of an early rest which no troubles can disturb, of a purity which no sin can stain, of a blessedness which no sorrow can mar, and of a glory which no cloud can darken. Till all this shall be attained let us labour on, hope on, pray on, and watch and struggle on, caring only that while a work of grace is fitting us for heaven, the gospel of grace may, through our being spent, be breaking forth to the glory of God and to the good of His Church, till the light affliction, which is but for a moment, shall have forever passed away."

Addresses were read out; one from the Presbytery of Inverness, one from the Free North Kirk Session, and one from the Free North congregation. The presentation of the Testimonial to Dr Mackay's long ministry was then made by Dr Mackenzie in a few well-chosen words and a presentation consisting of 853 sovereigns along with an inscribed silver plate was handed to the minister.

Dr Mackay then addressed the gathering by warmly thanking Dr Kennedy for presiding over this special occasion and warmly thanking the congregation and friends for their outstanding kindness to him.

In the course of his speech he said, "I have tried to minister as well as I could to the congregation since I came among them. I have tried to preach to them with great simplicity, and I trust that I have preached the true and pure theology – the old theology. Our respected Chairman can testify to that. I consider that the old wine is by far the best, and they will get nothing from me to the day of my death but the old wine. I never gave up the old wine, and my friend here at my right hand (Dr Mackenzie) has tried the old wine for a long, long time, and continues to take a glass of it every Sabbath day. I will never alter my conduct in regard to my preaching, and all my people know that I never had any idea of any other than the pure old theology."

As he drew to a close in his speech Dr Mackay introduced a sombre note and said, "A jubilee is a much more solemn thing to me than to any other person here. A jubilee implies fifty years, and a great many things occur in fifty years. There are a great many Sabbaths in fifty years; there are a great many sermons preached in fifty years; there are a great many souls gone into eternity in fifty years; there is a great deal of work that should be performed dutifully and faithfully in fifty years; and therefore it is a solemn consideration for a minister of the gospel the reflection that many, many who had heard him preach the gospel of Salvation had during fifty years gone to another world, their states being fixed in heaven or in hell. And the awful consideration teaches us to be faithful in our ministry for we are dealing with precious souls."

Speeches were made by Rev. Dr Donald Macdonald of Inverness High Church, Rev. Dr Gustavus Aird of Creich, William Simpson, Provost of Inverness, Rev. Malcolm Macgregor of Ferintosh, Rev. John Baillie of Gairloch, and others. The proceedings were brought to a close with various votes of thanks to all who made the evening an enjoyable success.

Throughout his long ministry in Inverness and when changes began to take place in the Church, he never deviated from his adherence to the Word of God. Another minister who celebrated his jubilee in the ministry about the same time as Dr Mackay was Rev. Harry Anderson of Partick Free Church. In his little volume called *Reminiscences of a Pastorate of Fifty Years* he recalls the wonderful days of Disruption times, as Mr. Mackay could. Anderson says, "I was always quickened by fellowship with Disruption ministers. I went up regularly to the General Assembly, somewhat like the Israelite who went up to Jerusalem, 'builded as a city that is compact together, whither the tribes go up, the tribes of the Lord unto the testimony of Israel.' The Free Church of Scotland was compactly built together then in her testimony for the King Jesus, in her Doctrine and her Faith. She was not pestered with attacks on the integrity, and Divine authority, and infallible Truth of the Word of God. No one whispered then about the need of a Declaratory Act to be used as a solvent to the Confession of Faith. Going to the General Assembly was like going to a Revival Meeting. But how changed are our assemblies now, with the disappearance of these Disruption Worthies. Dr Duff, the Indian Missionary, describes his feelings when he revisited Scotland and missed the familiar forms he had been wont to see: 'I felt as if I had entered a realm of sepulchres. A feeling of indescribable loneliness crept over my spirit.'"

The first twenty years of the Free Church were years of blessing and comparative harmony. In 1863, however, when the first union controversy began, an element of discord was introduced into a once united Church. At that time there were three major Presbyterian Churches in Scotland. There was the Established Church of Scotland, the Free Church of Scotland, and the United Presbyterian Church of Scotland. After a great deal of thought it was considered that a union of the Free and United Presbyterian Churches would be good for the cause of true religion in Scotland and to begin with there was enthusiasm for it. However, it soon became apparent that there were major differences between the Churches and to unite with a pseudo-Calvinistic Church would be disastrous for the Free Church.

Another matter that caused discord among brethren in the Free Church was the Praise Question. The Church had been an exclusive Psalm Singing Church but agitation now arose for the introduction of other items of praise and for the introduction of musical instruments.

The younger scholars of the Free Church also began to question the infallibility of the Word of God and were influenced by such critics of the Bible as K. H. Graf, Julius Wellhausen, and Abraham Kuenen.

Agitation had also begun to alter the strict adherence to the *Westminster Confession of Faith* which the ordination vow entailed, by introducing a Declaratory Act which would circumvent one's commitment to the Confession.

The Free Church was now like a once great, mighty ship which was at the mercy of a storm over which it had no control, and it was now only a matter of time before she would founder on the rock of unbelief.

Men like Dr Mackay began to feel the strain. The great men of the past were gone to their eternal rest such as Thomas Chalmers, William

Cunningham, James Buchanan, James Begg, John Kennedy, and other likeminded stalwarts of the Free Church. Sometimes Dr Mackay would say "You see I'm an old man. I don't care for all these controversies. I'm longing for the rest."

During the last four years of his life he had an assistant but that did not prevent him from performing ministerial duties and it was while attending a funeral service that he caught a chill which was for him the beginning of the end. He soon took to his bed but he had a premonition that death was near. He would say, "I'm tired of this world." In his prayers words of Scripture were never far from his lips and one of the last texts he repeated was, "They shall hunger no more, neither thirst any more; neither shall the sun light on them, nor any heat, etc." (Revelation 7:16-17).

Dr George Mackay passed away peacefully on the 27th June, 1886, in his ninetieth year. His body was laid to rest in the Chapel Yard, Inverness, in a spot not far from where he often preached in the open air to the Gaelic section of the congregation at the June communion. A stone marks his resting place, and a memorial tablet can be seen in the vestibule of the present Free North building alongside those commemorating the ministries of Rev. Archibald Cook and Rev. Murdo Mackenzie.

A little book printed by the *Inverness Courier* in 1889, called 'Biographies of Highland Clergymen' contains an appreciation of Dr George Mackay, and it is from this source the following quote comes. "For many long years the name of Rev. Dr George Mackay had been an influence and power in the Highlands. The clear-cut massive head, with the lofty brow and the snow-white hair, was a welcome sight in every pulpit in which it appeared. Dr Mackay was the last – or the last but one – of the race of Highland ministers whom the people implicitly revered and obeyed. In his latter days he was like the landmark of a past generation – the venerable survivor of an age which the modern flood was rapidly submerging." It goes on to say, "His attachments were strong and lasting; his efforts and his influences were exerted on behalf of truth and righteousness. In appearance he was spare, erect, and firm. Even in his ninetieth year, though his cheek had lost its roundness, his eye retained much of its old fire, and his form was almost unbent. Precise and neat in dress, and polite in manner, he looked what he was, a courteous, venerable gentleman, with a strong individuality. He has left his impress deep on the hearts of several generations of his hearers, and many a Highlander in distant lands heard of his death with sorrow."[28]

[28] *Biographies of Highland Clergymen*, pp. 102, 108.

CHAPTER 3

MURDO MACKENZIE

THE MAN who succeeded George Mackay in the North Church came from Lochcarron. Murdo Mackenzie was born on the 18th of August, 1835. His parents were God fearing and they lived in a small house in the centre of Lochcarron village. He was the youngest of seven children and was born with a slight deformity called torticollis, otherwise known as 'wry-neck' when the head appeared to rest on his left shoulder.

His father died when he had barely reached his fourth birthday and the widow with her young family left the village and moved to a place called Rhunesoul which lies on the shore of Loch Kishorn. Here he went to the local school where the young folks knew no English and where, in order to correct this, they were forbidden to speak Gaelic during school hours. When thirteen years old he moved to Inverness to further his education, and throughout his stay in the town he attended the North Church whose minister was Dr George Mackay. Little did the boy realise that one day he would become the great man's successor and that his own impact upon Inverness and the Free Church in general would be considerable. After schooldays he taught for a while in Kiltarlity and when eighteen years old he entered King's College, Aberdeen. After his Arts course he proceeded to study at the Free Church Divinity Halls in Glasgow and then in Edinburgh.

After his college course he suffered a breakdown in health which his wife tells us was brought on by overwork in his studies. This period of illness, however, turned out to be a memorable and profitable time for him. He was sent to Skye and spent three years with Alexander M'Coll who was then minister of Duirinish Free Church. M'Coll was a Lochcarron man and was the last child to be baptised by the famous Lachlan Mackenzie, otherwise known as 'Mr Lachlan.' It is recorded that as the father was handing back the child to its mother after its baptism, Mr Lachlan said "Thoir an deadh aire air an leanabh, bithidh e air fathast na lochran dealrach leis an Tighearn," which translated is: "Take good care of the child: he will yet be a shining light of the Lord." Lachlan Mackenzie is buried in the old Lochcarron cemetery and his grave is near the remaining walls of the church where many were brought to Christ under his warm evangelical preaching. Among his converts was Kate Mor, a woman well advanced in years and whose sinful life caused her such tears of penitence that her eyesight was affected. In fulfilment of Mr. Lachlan's prophecy her grave is not far from her minister's. M'Coll served the Free Church in Applecross before his ordination and induction to Duirinish in 1852. Later in 1870, he became Free Church minister of Fort Augustus and Glenmoriston, and then, from 1877 until his death in 1889, he was minister of Lochalsh.

In an age of outstanding Highland preachers, M'Coll has been described as "a spiritual star of the first magnitude." He had a fine presence, a good voice, and an impressive pulpit manner. Wherever he went he drew people to him and some compared him not unfavourably with John MacDonald, the 'Apostle of the North,' while others with Dr John Kennedy of Dingwall. Like Kennedy he seems to have had insights into "the secret of the Lord," and warned people of "things that must shortly come to pass." For example, he foretold God's judgment upon industrial Clydeside for its flagrant disobedience of the fourth commandment and seemed to indicate that the judgment would be in the form of commercial impoverishment. At any rate, most of the great shipyards which once employed thousands of workers lie silent. And today the famous river Clyde which once bustled with shipping is dead in comparison with what it was. Small ferry boats, a number of cargo ships, and the pleasure yachts of the rich have replaced the great liners and the giant cargo vessels which plied the ports with trade. M'Coll also prayed that those engaged in the construction of the Benedictine monastery at Fort Augustus might not succeed and as long as he lived the work was either retarded or brought to a standstill. Today the building has for the present been abandoned as a monastery.

Mackenzie learned from this pious man what it means to live close to God. He also inherited from him a love of Thomas Goodwin, the Puritan, who was a favourite writer with M'Coll. Later in his ministry, Mackenzie acknowledged, "Under God, any success I have had in my ministry is due to Thomas Goodwin." In appreciation of the Duirinish minister, Mackenzie named one of his daughters, Alexandrina, after him.

In October 1863, Murdo Mackenzie was licensed to preach by the Presbytery of Lochcarron and for a short time thereafter he assisted the Rev. Hugh Mackay of Kilmun near Dunoon. In 1870 he received a call from the congregation of Kilcalmonell, Argyllshire, which he accepted, and on October 5th, 1870, he was ordained and inducted to the charge. The Church is situated in the picturesque village of Clachan. His first ministry was to be of short duration but during it, he made many friends, one of whom was Sir William Mackinnon, a friend of the Constitutional party of the pre-1900 Free Church. In 1873 the congregation of Kilmallie addressed to Mr. Mackenzie a unanimous call and although the Clachan people pled with him to remain with them, he yielded to the request of the Kilmallie congregation.

Kilmallie, which lies in the shadow of Ben Nevis, offered Mackenzie a wider sphere of service. It was part of Gaeldom, and here he could feel at home and exercise his ministry in Gaelic, as well as in English. Here too, he could enjoy the catechising meetings which were still part of Highland church life. These catechising gatherings served a twofold purpose. They were useful for district visitation of the congregation and enabled pastor and people to become acquainted with one another. They also served for instructing the people in Bible Knowledge and Doctrine and helped the minister to assess the spiritual strengths and weaknesses of his flock, and thereby he could accommodate his preaching to their needs.

During his ministry, Kilmallie flourished under the preaching of the gospel, and his dynamic leadership earned him a respected place in the esteem of his brethren throughout the Free Church. Summer Gaelic communion services were generally held in the open air on a hillside not far from Loch Linnhe. And here, under the preaching of men like John Kennedy of Dingwall, Alexander M'Coll of Lochalsh, Gustavus Aird of Creich, and other Gaelic worthies, the gospel would be proclaimed from a wooden construction called 'The Tent' while the crowds gathered around and were seated on benches or on the heather. The Kilmallie people became attached to him and from time to time they expressed their appreciation and affection in a tangible way. He also won the confidence of the community in general by being elected to the School Board which was then regarded as a position of prestige and importance in the local community. Principal John Macleod who knew the area well in his boyhood, in his book *By-paths of Highland Church History*, gives his estimate of the worth of the man. He writes, "The palmy days of the Free Church in Kilmallie were during the ministry of the Rev. Murdo Mackenzie, 1873-87. He was a master of assemblies, and he kept the affairs of the congregation in the best of order. His mother wit, his homely ways, and his powerful and rousing preaching, along with his frank outspokenness, made him the very minister for the people."[29]

After a ministry in Kilmallie of almost fifteen years the call from the Free North Church, Inverness came to him in 1887, and on 9th September of that year he was inducted to the charge. The Highland capital was different from Kilmallie. The level of work was greater: for in the town he had to preach three times every Lord's Day, visit a congregation of more

---

[29] Macleod, *By-paths of Highland Church History*, p. 67.

than 2,000 people, perform innumerable baptisms, marriages, and funerals, to say nothing of the added work of assisting at other communion services, and acting for the wider Church as a visiting delegate. All this, along with the strain of the 1900 Church crisis, required him to have had a strong constitution, and even he began to feel the effects of the intolerable pressure.

On 26th of August, 1886, when just turned fifty years of age, Murdo Mackenzie married Ella Stewart Shaw, the only daughter of the Rev. Dugald Shaw, the Free Church minister of Laggan. Dugald Shaw was a good man who wrote the biography of a worthy woman, *Isabella MacFarlane of Strathbraan*, a book which reveals Shaw's evangelical

sympathies. His daughter, Ella, was an accomplished young woman. The Mackenzies had a family of five daughters and one son; one of the daughters died when only eleven months old, and another when in her early teens. Mrs Mackenzie was a good minister's wife. She kept a watchful eye on the congregation and gathered around her a group of young ladies who often met at the manse as a sewing class.

When Murdo Mackenzie arrived in Inverness, preparations were well underway for holding the 1888 Free Church General Assembly in the town. It had been agreed the previous year that the time had come to hold the Free Church Assembly in the Highland capital and that it should be presided over by a Highland moderator. The necessary arrangements required a great deal of work to be done and a steering committee made up of ministers and office bearers from local Free Church congregations was formed to progress the work. A wooden building designed along the lines of the Assembly Hall in Edinburgh was constructed on an open space in Ardross Terrace. The hall was seated for up to 3,000 people. It had various committee rooms as well as a refreshment room. Necessary furniture such as the Moderator's chair and desk, along with the Clerk's table and other items had to be transported from Edinburgh so that members of Assembly felt quite at home in the Inverness hall. Since Dr George Mackay and Dr John Kennedy had passed away, the choice of moderator fell upon Dr Gustavus Aird of Creich who commanded the respect of Free Church people in the south as well as the north. He was a Disruption veteran who had signed the *Act of Separation and Deed of Demission* and he ably discharged the duties of the office with becoming dignity and efficiency.

A memorial volume which gives an account of the entire proceedings of that Assembly was published by the *Courier* Office in 1888. It includes Dr Aird's opening address on, 'The Progress of Religion in the North since the time of the Reformation,' and his concluding speech on 'The Social Condition of the People.' These addresses did ample justice to their themes for no man had a greater grasp of Highland Church history and the problems of Highland social life, than the venerable Moderator. On the Wednesday afternoon of that memorable week, Dr Aird was presented with the Freedom of the Burgh of Inverness by the Provost, Sir H. C. MacAndrew, in recognition of the esteemed place which Dr Aird held in his Church, and also in recognition of the Free Church of Scotland by honouring the town in this particular way.

When Mackenzie took up the pastorate in Inverness the question of the old building on North Place had to be addressed. The North Church had been built in 1837 and it was a plain Georgian box styled building with narrow pews designed for numbers rather than comfort. Towards the end of Dr Mackay's ministry, it had been agreed to replace the church and a building fund was set up. The mammoth task, however, was too much for the old minister who was now nearly ninety years of age. The new minister was in his prime and with an enthusiastic band of office bearers the task was addressed. In July 1889 a committee was formed to advance the undertaking. A site had to be procured for the new building and as the manse on Church Street had a garden of considerable size where better to build than on the garden site.

The architect chosen to design the building was Sir Alexander Ross whose home was called 'Riverfield', which was situated on Island Bank Road. He was a public-spirited man who served for a time as Provost of the town. As an architect he gained for himself a distinguished reputation and his work is to be seen in a number of public buildings in the town. His style is Gothic. His most impressive work is the Episcopal Cathedral on the west side of the river which was opened in 1866. He also designed St John's Episcopal Church, opened in 1891. The design which he chose for the new North building was similar to the Free High Church on Bank Street which is now called St Columba Church of Scotland.

The Church had to seat what was then the largest congregation in the town and so its proportions required to be considerable. The impressive frontage is 67 feet across and its length is 163 feet. It had comfortable seating for 1,400. The dominating feature of the building is the massive spire which rises to a height of 170 feet and is taller than the steeples of the old High Church, the Burgh, and the Cathedral. The cost of the steeple alone was £1,200 of which £1,000 was contributed by Mrs MacGillivray, a lady of considerable means.

The interior impresses one with its cathedral like dimensions. There is a barrel vault roof giving the impression of vastness, the three large galleries; one in the centre facing the pulpit, and the other two on the side walls. A most distinguishing feature is the high pulpit with the precentor's desk below it, and below that again the lectern where the elders used to sit. "The great size of the pulpit," writes Campbell Mackenzie, "and the profusion of crockets and finials tend to dwarf the preacher, to prevent too much attention being paid to the man, although, as he stands at the reading desk, a roundel at the back of the chair lines up with his head, –

creating a halo effect." All the woodwork is pitch pine. Eight doors give ample access to and from the main auditorium and galleries, and along with the six main doors opening on to Bank Street, Church Lane, and Church Street, allow for quick exit from the building should that be required. There is also a large hall, two smaller halls, a spacious kitchen, and a vestry. The new building was an achievement and reflects credit on the minister, office bearers, and people of the day, who built it for the glory of God and the preaching of the gospel.

A criticism made on the occasion of its opening and which appeared in a *Courier* report at the time is still valid. "One is almost tempted to regret, however, that such a handsome structure is not situated in a locality where its massive dimensions and architectural grace could be seen to more advantage. Handsome though the Church is, it looks cabined and confined on its present low-lying situation with buildings crowding in upon either side of it." Another criticism is that the pulpit is too high and too remote from the people because the nearer they sit forward the more they have to crane their necks to look up to the preacher and such a posture creates discomfort. These criticisms apart; it is an impressive building with good acoustics. The total sum involved in its construction was £11,000.

The memorial stone was laid by Sir William Mackinnon on 11th September, 1891, and the building was officially opened on Wednesday the 7th of June, 1893. It was a notable occasion. The morning Gaelic service began at 11 am when Dr Aird of Creich preached an impressive sermon from Psalm 63, verse 2, "To see thy power and thy glory, so as I have seen thee in the sanctuary." At 1.30 pm there was an English service conducted by Dr Alexander Mackenzie, of the Free Tolbooth Church in Edinburgh, who preached an eloquent sermon from Revelation, chapter 1, verses 17 and 18: "Fear not; I am the first and the last: I am he that liveth, and was dead; and, behold, I am alive for evermore, Amen; and have the keys of hell and of death." In the evening the Church was crowded to hear the Rev. Murdo MacAskill of Dingwall preach a powerful sermon from Psalm 87, verse 3, "Glorious things are spoken of thee, O city of God." And so, the Church began a new chapter in its history.

Aden House was purchased in 1892 and became the new manse. It cost £1,500 and £100 was spent on it to make it a suitable home for the Mackenzies. It was a prestigious Victorian house set on the then outskirts of the town and in open country. Nearby on Argyll Street there was a farm where the present Crown Vets veterinary practice is, and the old cobble stones of the farmyard are still there. The cattle used to be taken along Southside Place, past Aden House to the fields opposite the manse to graze. The extensive grounds surrounding the house were kept in proper order by the gardener, and croquet would sometimes be played on the lawn.

The Free Church of the nineties was no longer the Free Church of the fifties and sixties. The conservatism of early days was fast disappearing as the Disruption Fathers and their immediate successors passed from the scene and were replaced by a younger generation of ministers conditioned by the supposedly advanced but unbelieving learning of the times. The spiritual strength and power of early days had given way to a spiritually bankrupt intellectualism. Instead of faithful discipline being exercised upon erring brethren, the Church pursued a policy of evasion and accommodation which was ultimately to lead to her undoing. Professor William Robertson Smith, who had disseminated Higher Critical views on the Old Testament among his students, was removed from his position by the General Assembly in 1881. Others, however, who should have been removed for heresy, were allowed to remain in their offices such as Dr Marcus Dods and Dr Alexander B. Bruce, who were tried in 1890 but were inexplicably exonerated from the charges laid against them. Murdo Mackenzie was a member of that Assembly and he made it plain where he stood. Addressing Dr Dods' statement in a sermon preached in St Giles that "we must not too hastily conclude that even belief in Christ's divinity is essential to a true Christian," Mackenzie asked the Assembly: Was that the gospel which the great Head of the Church and which the Free Church of Scotland commissioned him to go and preach to his people? He went on to say, "He had a church which was as crowded as that Assembly, and if he preached the doctrine of the St Giles' sermon his church would soon be empty, and the sooner by such preaching it was empty the better." He continued, "Was the teaching of the St Giles' sermon the kind of teaching that Dr Pierson would wish taught by men who went to preach the everlasting gospel to the ends of the earth? Would he ask him to go forward and preach that it was not essential in order to be a true Christian to believe in the divinity of our Lord? He maintained that that was a false Christ. That statement in Dr Dods' sermon took away from him his Lord, and he did not know where he had laid Him. Where was their hope for eternity if they went with such statements as these to their people? They would be leading them in the wrong way, making a false profession, and building upon a foundation of sand."[30] The day, however, for dealing firmly with heresy was over, and Dods went on to become Principal of New College, in succession to Dr Robert Rainy, in 1907.

Another matter which grieved Murdo Mackenzie was the *Declaratory Act* which came before the Church courts and which was passed into legislation in 1893. He was vehemently opposed to it and along with other constitutionalists maintained that "so long as the subscription to the Confession remained unaltered, he regarded it [the *Declaratory Act*] as a dead letter."[31]

Some fifty people left the North Church to join the new Free Presbyterian Church. After a time, some who had left returned and he was informed that a certain individual would come back if asked to do so by the minister. Mackenzie's reaction was typical, "I never asked him to leave; the door is open if he wished to return." Although Mackenzie never took cognisance of the new Free Presbyterian Church, he remained friendly to those who left to join it. In November 1911, when a prominent member of the Free Presbyterian Church died, Mackenzie attended his funeral. Shortly afterwards, the following letter from the deceased's son-in-law was received, kept, and treasured by Mackenzie:

---

[30] Murdo Mackenzie, *Autobiography*, p. 79.
[31] As above, pp. 187-8.

Rev. Dear Sir,

I desire, on behalf of my wife and myself, to sincerely thank you for your kindness in attending my father-in-law's funeral on Tuesday last. I would have taken an earlier opportunity of writing, but was unable to do so through illness. I actually rose from a sick bed to attend the funeral.

I have a communication to make to you, and it is one which I as a medium have much pleasure in doing, knowing the friendship which so closely existed and so many associations between you as minister and the late Mr M. in former days – and that they did not continue, I fully know, was due to no fault or action of yours.

This being so, it is, I think, all the more gratifying that he should frequently express himself very clearly on the matter, and a few days before he died, when words came slowly and at intervals, but yet with conspicuous clearness, he said in Gaelic, of which the following is the actual translation, "Although we have been separate from each other for years, owing to church differences, still my heart is as tied to him as in the old days, and my heart would rejoice once more to see him before I die, and I wish you to tell him so."

Nothing was possible, as shortly thereafter, instead of reviving, he rapidly got weaker, and passed peacefully away on Saturday.

Yours faithfully, FGF

The years leading up to the 1900 union were distressing and stressful for the constitutionalists; nevertheless, Murdo Mackenzie worked tirelessly for his Church and particularly for his congregation. In 1892 he was appointed a representative by the General Assembly to the Pan-Presbyterian Council being held at Toronto in Canada. He enjoyed the beauty of the parts of Canada and North America which he visited, and was impressed by the Niagara Falls. Most of all he enjoyed meeting the migrant Highlanders who, although they had made their homes in the west, still loved their native Gaelic culture and enjoyed church services in their mother tongue. Many came to see and hear him and to enquire of relatives whom they were sure were known to the popular minister from Inverness.

Murdo Mackenzie was not in the habit of taking an annual holiday but a severe attack of rheumatism in 1897 called for respite from the pressure of work. In the spring of that year he travelled to Jerusalem and visited many places recorded in Bible history, such as Mamre, Hebron, Bethlehem, the field of Boaz, the wilderness of Judea, the Dead Sea, the Jordan, the Brook Kerith, Bethany, and so on. The return journey home took him through Italy, France via Paris, and on to London and Inverness.[32] It had the effect of reinvigorating and preparing him for further work in his Master's service.

He was a methodical man, a wise administrator, and a gifted preacher. Sabbath was his busy day when he conducted three services, one in Gaelic in the morning, an English one in the afternoon and another English one in the evening. The distance from church to manse was considerable and time consuming for a man who was advancing in years and rather than climb Castle Street more than once on a Sunday he preferred to stay in the church in between the services and rest. His preaching was greatly appreciated in both Gaelic and English and his fine voice and excellent delivery carried his message to the four corners of the massive building. That was no mean task in days before a voice amplification system was introduced. His commanding presence too made him an impressive sight in the pulpit. Communion was dispensed twice in the year, generally on the last Sabbaths of January and June. The Gaelic services were held in the Church and the English services in the hall. The summer Gaelic communion was dispensed, weather permitting, in the Chapel Yard (the cemetery opposite John Fraser, the undertaker) and for twenty-one years, Mr Mackenzie conducted this service until it was banned by Inverness Town Council in 1909. It was estimated according to the number of coins put in the offering plate at the gate of the cemetery that the congregation would number in the region of 2,000. 'The Tent', or wooden pulpit, was sent up at the wall not far from where Dr George Mackay's grave is. The

---

[32] This is described in his wife's biography of her husband: *Murdo Mackenzie: A Memory* (Inverness, 1914), pp. 137-183.

long communion tables and the rows of forms were placed in front of the pulpit. Some of these old seat forms were, until recently, kept in the tunnel that runs from the front of the church to the back entrance on Church Lane. Sometimes town people wandered into this open-air place of worship and sat either on the grass or the flat tombstones and listened to the inspired Gaelic psalm singing led by a good precentor who would chant the verses line by line while the congregation would follow him and, in Mrs Mackenzie's words, "as the waves of sad or triumphal melody rose and fell, and again re-echoed from the outskirts of the multitude it was a diapason of Highland melody, a truly spiritual service of song."

The interests of Mr Mackenzie were wide and broad. He had a love for young people and it was a great joy for him to see them from their earliest days gathering under the sound of the gospel. There was a large Sunday School in the North Church under a capable leader and his devoted band of teachers. An annual soirée was held in January. The word 'soir' comes from the French meaning evening, and the soirée was really an evening party with tea. The young folks with their parents would gather in the hall, and after the opening preliminaries tea would be served with a bag of buns for the young people. To youngsters the bag was full of mystery and it would be opened with great excitement to see if there was at least one iced bun inside. After tea there were recitals when a boy or girl would be called upon to do a recitation, quote a poem, or sing a psalm or a hymn. The proceedings ended with praise and prayer. Usually there was a summer outing.

A Mutual Improvement Society was initiated in 1886. This society, which was for the benefit of helping young men to address the problems of the day, was not exclusive to the Free North: there were similar societies held in other Free Church congregations throughout Scotland. Copies of the syllabus of those years show how lively the organisation was in the North Church. The minister was the Honorary President. There was a president, two vice presidents, a secretary, a treasurer, joint conveners, and members of committee. Subjects discussed were varied and based on such themes as literature, the old age pension scheme, life assurance, scientific matters, athletics, and there were lively debates and discussions, as well as social evenings. It was a popular meeting for young men and well patronised by them. There was also a Young Women's Sewing Class which met at the manse under the supervision of Mrs Mackenzie. She was a gifted lady who was greatly admired by the young women who surrounded her and she could not but influence them for good. The manse pew was the back seat in the right-hand corner of the lane side of the Church facing the side of the pulpit. From that corner seat she kept a watchful eye and noted absentees so that minister and office bearers were informed and such absentees would be visited to see if there was anything seriously amiss in their homes.

Another matter in which Murdo Mackenzie was deeply interested was Foreign Missions, and under his leadership the congregation became noted for its support of that work. He became a great supporter of The China Inland Mission. One day in Kilmallie, while reading the first chapter of Amos, he stopped and said, "Amos was called when he was doing his ordinary work among the herdsmen of Tekoa. Is there no one here who will consecrate himself to the Foreign Mission Field?" There was a response to that call. James Stewart, an elder's son, at the close of the service said he would like to go. When he asked his minister about the means that would be required, Mackenzie assured him, "The Lord will provide." James Stewart trained as a medical missionary and during his first furlough home Dr Stewart stayed at Aden House and inspired the congregation and created an interest among them in the work of the China Inland Mission. For fourteen years quantities of woollen garments along with financial donations were sent every New Year in support of the work. Another field in which the congregation helped was the mission work at Livingstonia, and even after it came under the jurisdiction of the United Free Church it continued to be supported by the Free North congregation. It was Professor T. M. Lindsay of the Free Church College in Glasgow, when convener of the Foreign Missions Committee, who said, "if we had a Murdo Mackenzie in every parish, there would be no fear of the Foreign Mission collection." Mackenzie used to tell of the poor Lewis woman who consecrated a hen to Foreign Missions. All the profit from the eggs went to the collector. "The Saviour," he would say, "left two commands, which are the special heritage of his disciples in all ages – 'This do in remembrance of me,' and 'Go ye into all the world and preach the gospel to every creature,' and he would add, 'A congregation with no missionary zeal is dead.'"

Friendship meant much to him and it grieved him when church disputes created unpleasantness. But he never allowed divisions to come between him and those who were his brethren in Christ Jesus. For example, he and the Earl of Moray had been good friends and at General Assemblies they would sit and vote together. Indeed, when the Earl visited him in Kilmallie and later in Inverness on communion occasions, the nobleman helped at these services in the capacity of an elder. When the Earl died in 1901, Murdo Mackenzie spoke with deep emotion from the North pulpit of the Earl's attachment to the Free Church and of the happy communion gatherings of the past, and he went on to say, "Oh! These miserable divisions of ours which threaten to mar, and in many cases to render impossible altogether, these gatherings together in Christian fellowship which had so many hallowed associations." He and Dr Black of the Free High Church in Inverness were the best of friends and although on opposite sides at the 1900 union they remained firm friends. When Dr Black died suddenly in 1907, Murdo Mackenzie was visibly moved when making reference to his former comrade, from the North pulpit.

Rev. Murdo MacAskill was another old friend who had for years been a leading opponent of the union negotiations but who eventually defected and in 1900 joined the United Free Church. But that did not alter Murdo Mackenzie's esteem of his friend. When MacAskill became unwell and died in 1903 the North minister visited him and took part in his funeral service.

From 1900, until his death in 1912, Murdo Mackenzie carried on with his work as a Free Church minister and held his large congregation together. In 1901 the United Free Presbytery formally declared the North

Church vacant. An old adherent's reaction on hearing the news was, "Vacant indeed! And it packed to the door!", and so it continued. The rupture of the Free Church in 1900 pained him and like the others of that goodly band of constitutionalists he missed the large church and friends from whom he was parted by the union. In the immediate post union years he took little to do with the litigation that proceeded. If fault is to be found with him, it is surely in this matter, for had Colin Bannatyne, James Duff MacCulloch, John Kennedy Cameron, and others held back, as he did, there would have been no Free Church today. However, as the years passed he saw it to be his duty to help the small struggling congregations in the Inverness Presbytery, and after much persuasion he eventually accepted the Moderatorship of the Free Church of Scotland Assembly in 1907. In 1902 he attended the Conference of Psalm Singers in Belfast.[33] In 1909 he was made a delegate to the Pan Presbyterian Council in New York and on that occasion he was accompanied by his son.

There were the dark shadows that cast their gloom over him. He and his wife were blessed with four daughters and one son. One of the daughters died in infancy and then in 1909 Alexandrina, the youngest, after returning from school in the south developed acute peritonitis. She died in the manse shortly after being operated on. He never recovered from her death. Sometimes he dreamt of things that were about to happen and would inform his wife of them. An illustration of this involved his friend, Sir William Mackinnon, who stood for Parliament. Mackenzie dreamt that a huge tree in front of Mackinnon's house fell with a mighty crash. He interpreted the dream as Mackinnon losing the vote, and so it happened. Prior to his daughter's death he dreamed that floods of water poured out of Aden House followed by a white coffin. The floods of water indicated many tears. That was a dream which he never related to his wife until after the event.

---

[33] For Murdo Mackenzie's address at this conference, 'The Singing of Praise: Its Divine Authority and Objects', see *Psalm-Singers' Conference, Belfast, August, 1902* (Belfast, 1903), pp. 19-22.

Until his death in 1912 he held his large congregation together and throughout the Edwardian years when modernism in the pulpit was becoming increasingly fashionable, he continued to preach with the same evangelical fervour as before. What an inspiring sight in those days to see the building filled to capacity, with pews crowded with people, young and old.

Let us go down memory lane, and join Professor Alexander Ross as he recalls what it was like in the summers of 1910-11 when he was a student assistant. In his 'Random Memories' which he contributed to *The Monthly Record* in the early 1960s, he writes, "I have never forgotten the sensation of something very like panic which almost overwhelmed me, when that vast congregation rose up for the first prayer. But I was wonderfully held up by a strength not my own, and, once I had, so to speak, found my feet, I discovered in the great gatherings, a mighty inspiration, and the grand singing, under the leadership of Mr William Simpson, was a mighty inspiration also, as good singing is to a preacher. We had some never-to-be forgotten Sabbath evenings in the Free North during those summers of the long ago." Nor is it difficult to visualise Murdo Mackenzie, who is described by Professor Collins as "that outstanding preacher," bending over the pulpit and pleading with his fellow mortals in his own winsome way to be reconciled to God through Christ the Saviour. His wife tells us that he would say, "Will you not come now, while He is waiting to be gracious? If you do not come, Oh! remember that the curse of the gospel is more terrible than the curse of the law. If you do not believe in Christ, we are not sons but slaves. Slaves of sin and of Satan. Oh! flee to Jesus now that it is the day of salvation. He is waiting for you." And he would cry in that authoritative and commanding way of his, "Open your heart to the Saviour before the grave opens its mouth for you, for there is no work, nor device, nor knowledge, nor wisdom, in the grave, whither thou goest."

Mr Mackenzie continued his pulpit work until February, 1911, when by that time he was far from well. He died the following year, on Sabbath morning May 26th, 1912. His wife writes, "The Master Builder, having

60

finished the mansion for His servant, sent his angels to fetch him, and we who watched heard their wondrous song. The tense silence which followed – during which I felt uncertain as to whether I was in the body or not – was broken by our dear old nurse saying – 'You heard the singing?'"[34]

The funeral was from the Free North Church to Tomnahurich cemetery. A large procession followed the cortege made up of chief mourners, representatives of the Council, representatives of the various churches, and a detachment of the Cameron Highlanders. Large crowds lined the route. Murdo Mackenzie was laid to rest in the plot of ground at the top of Tomnahurich where his daughters lie buried, and there the body rests until the resurrection. Murdo Mackenzie was a strong and powerful character who left an indelible mark upon the church scene in his day.

After his death Mrs Mackenzie and her family moved to London to a house called 'Lanrig', Canonbie Road, Forest Hill. Before the Misses Noble of Ardross Street passed away, they handed to the writer a letter dated 22nd August, 1912, from Mrs Mackenzie, part of which reads,

> My dear Katie,
>
> You, and all my dear girls, will like to know that we are now quite settled in our new home. It is very different from Inverness but it is a charming little place. You would all like it, I know. It is on a hill and there is a lovely view of London in the distance. St Paul's Cathedral, and Tower Bridge, and Westminster. There is a tiny garden in front and quite a nice little croquet green behind, with a flower plot round and plum trees. A nice summer house where, when the weather permits, we have tea – at the end. The dining room has a French window which opens like a door, which is nice…We have not quite decided which church to join. The Scotch Church is very nice but it is further away than the North Church was. All the same I think we shall probably go there. It was nice to see the Burning Bush once more and last Sabbath we sang the 34th Psalm to Irish. I hope your father keeps well. Give my love to all the girls – and say I do not forget them as you all know…I

---

[34] Ella S. Mackenzie, *Murdo Mackenzie: A Memory* (Inverness, 1914), p. 252.

am still very tired and have had to rest in bed some days. Perhaps you will read this to the girls dear? at least to those who were longest with me.

Your affectionate friend,

Ella S. Mackenzie."

Mrs Mackenzie died in London early in 1922. A minute appears in the Kirk Session record of 20th February, 1922, which states, "The Session agreed to send a letter of condolence to Mr Murdo Mackenzie, Grey's Hospital, London, as representing the family of the late pastor in connection with their recent bereavement in the loss of their mother, Mrs Mackenzie."

A memorial plaque with the following inscription was placed in the wall of the vestibule of the North Church alongside those commemorating his predecessors, – Rev. A. Cook and Dr G. Mackay.

The esteem in which Rev. Murdo Mackenzie was held by his congregation, and the people of the Highlands in general, was well expressed in the impressive and eloquent minute of the Kirk Session of the 4th June, 1912. It reads:

> The Kirk Session desire to record in their minutes the deep-felt loss sustained by the congregation, by the community, and by the people of the Highlands at large, by his removal. For nearly twenty-five years, he presided over the deliberations of this court with conspicuous loyalty to his Divine Master, and to the eternal interests of his flock. He brought to bear upon all the work of the court the gift of a sharp intellect, the sanctified wisdom of ripened years and the invaluable experience of intimate fellowship with his Lord. In all the functions of his sacred office to which in God's good providence he was called, he showed himself a servant worthy of his vocation in his illuminated exposition of Scripture, in his direct messages, proceeding from a soul aglow with earnestness for the salvation of his fellow men, in his impressive appeals and his solemn warnings, he faithfully discharged his commission as an ambassador of Christ in the greatest of all services, pleading with sinners to be reconciled to God.

The session record with heartfelt gratitude to God, his tender sympathy in the homes of affliction, his cheering and comforting counsels to the souls entering the eternal world, his kindly candour and affectionate remonstrance with the careless, as well as his pious demeanour in the houses of his flock; with no less gratitude would they recall his valued services in all that affected the moral wellbeing of the community in all that tended to uplift the citizens in all that made for righteousness in this town and surroundings. No more striking proof of his valuable and appreciated public services could be evinced than the unprecedented display of sympathy expressed by the funeral procession, consisting of representatives of all the Public Bodies in the town in their corporate capacity, which followed the remains through a dense and deeply affected crowd of people, to their last resting place.

His services in the cause of Jesus Christ throughout the Highlands of Scotland have left their impress upon the character and religious life of not a few. His services to his own church which he adorned for over forty years of a truly successful ministry, shall remain a cherished memory of the devout and pious of the people.

Humbly and reverently would the Session bow their heads in this the hour of their affliction under the chastening hand of Him whose purposes concerning His people are ever holy and good, trusting that the All Wise One, who, when He calls away, is able also to call into the breach He has created; and with his hope and confidence, the Session commit their interests to the Chief Shepherd, praying that He may place over them an under shepherd, who may lead the flock in the green pastures of the truth, in the manner in which, in God's providence they have been guided and fed for the last five and twenty years.

The Session also desire to record their deepest sympathy with the widow and children of their late beloved pastor who, they pray, may be sustained in this their time of grief, while the consolations of the gospel of their blessed Lord, through the teaching of the Great Comforter, the Holy Spirit, may soothe and comfort them. They also direct that an excerpt of this minute be sent to the bereaved widow and family.

It was signed by John Fraser, the Clerk of Session.

CHAPTER 4

JOHN MACLEOD

THE MAN WHOSE NAME commended itself to the people of the Free North congregation on the death of Murdo Mackenzie was that of Alexander Stewart, who was then minister of Fountainbridge Free Church in Edinburgh.

Stewart was born at the head of Glen Glass, near Evanton, in 1870. He studied in both Aberdeen and Glasgow. In 1893 when the *Declaratory Act* was passed by an overwhelming majority in the pre-1900 Free Church it brought into existence the Free Presbyterian Church. Alexander Stewart, along with John Macleod, George Mackay, and other students identified themselves with the new protesting church. In 1898 Stewart was appointed minister of the Free Presbyterian Church in Oban. He was later translated to the congregation in Edinburgh. However, after the House of Lords decision in favour of the minority Free Church in 1904 and with the rescinding of the Declaratory Act along with other unconstitutional pre-1900 legislation, he, along with his congregation, saw it as his duty to return to the Free Church, thereby becoming minister of Fountainbridge Free Church, Edinburgh.

Alexander Stewart was a literary man and a gifted bi-lingual preacher. In 1906 he was appointed the first editor of the Church's children's magazine which was called, *The Instructor.* In 1917 he succeeded Archibald MacNeilage as editor of *The Monthly Record.* His books, *Jeremiah, the Man and his Message, Elisha, a Prophet of Grace,* and a posthumous work called *Shoes for the Road,* reflect his fine command of language along with an eloquent literary style. He also co-authored, along with Professor J. K. Cameron, *The Free Church of Scotland – the crisis of 1900.*[35] A series of lectures under the auspices of the Protestant Truth Society appeared in book form under the title, *Roman Dogma and Scripture Truth,* and was published in 1931. The honorary degree of Doctor of Divinity was conferred upon him by Glasgow University in 1926, the same year in which he was appointed Moderator of the General Assembly of the Free Church of Scotland. Principal John Macleod's assessment of him is given in these words, "Dr Stewart was a man of rare mental endowments. He had a great natural shrewdness and penetration, and his intellect was as comprehensive as it was clear. He wielded a facile pen, which gave easy and elegant expression to the thoughts of a remarkably well balanced mind."[36]

A call was signed in his favour by 1,437 persons, and after giving the matter serious and prayerful consideration it was declined in the foregoing gracious terms to the Free North Session Clerk:

> Dear Mr. Fraser,
>
> …The sphere of usefulness presented by so splendid a body of people, the traditions of the congregation, and its place of influence in the community all have been before my mind. Will you also believe me when I say that I have tried to place myself unreservedly in God's hands? For the last number of weeks, I have not thought or prayed about anything else. In these circumstances, I cherish the confidence that I am being led in the right way. The conclusion to which I have come, accordingly, is that apart altogether from the persuasion that the burden of the work in Inverness is somewhat beyond my strength, my mission in Edinburgh is not yet done." [He goes on to end his letter:] "I should also esteem it a favour if you would intimate somehow to the congregation the pain which it gives me to send this reply, and the

---

[35] First published in 1910 this volume was reissued by the Free Church of Scotland in 1989.
[36] John Macleod, Foreword in *Shoes for the Road*, pp. 5-6.

honour which I shall always count it to have been called to be their minister.

With kindest regards, I am, dear Mr. Fraser,

Yours very sincerely,

Alexander Stewart.

The congregation now considered the Rev. George Mackay of Fearn. In his heyday he was regarded as one of the best preachers in the Free Church. He had been the minister of Stornoway Free Church from 1906 to 1910, and then he was translated to Fearn Free Church. Mackay did not allow the Free North to proceed in the matter and so his name was dropped.

In October 1912 it was agreed by the vacancy committee to approach John Macleod who was Professor of Greek and New Testament in the Free Church College. A deputation was sent from Inverness to interview him but he pointed out that as he had been unanimously and cordially appointed to his important position by the General Assembly, he was directly responsible to the Supreme Court of the Church, and consequently would not feel free to change without receiving the sanction of that court. This report by the deputation was indeed a great disappointment to the vacancy committee and it was felt that it would be futile to pursue the matter further.

In February 1913, however, discussions were re-opened with Professor Macleod when he expressed his sympathy with the congregation in their predicament, and to prevent damage by division he offered whatever help he could. In a letter to the vacancy committee which appears in the Free North Kirk Session minutes he stated, "If satisfactory arrangements could be made to secure that the work of the Chair here should not suffer during a suspension of my tenancy of it, I should be willing to leave myself, as the servant of the church, in the hands of the General Assembly and if they think I am called to fill, D.V., the charge at Inverness for a period of three, four, or five years, I should not refuse to obey a definite indication of their mind."

Positive steps were now taken and a call was addressed to him which contained 1,579 signatures of people over the age of eighteen. A petition was sent to the General Assembly of 1913 craving his release from his College duties and that the call from Inverness be placed in his hands. After deliberating on the matter and by a narrow margin of votes it was agreed to release him from his Chair and translate him to Inverness. The reluctance on the part of so many of his brethren to his translation was obvious: his services to the Free Church College were invaluable and he could ill be spared in the training of students for the ministry. On the 23rd of July 1913 he was inducted to the Free North Church.

John Macleod was born in Fort William on the 25th day of March 1872 and was baptised in the Free Church. He grew up under the ministry of the Rev. Charles Stewart who was a good man but by no means an inspiring preacher. It was the influence of his God-fearing parents that made an indelible impression upon his mind. On Sunday mornings his mother used to quote the lines: "This is the day when Jesus rose, so early from the dead. Why should I keep my eyelids closed and waste my hours in bed? This is the day when Jesus broke the power of death and hell. Why should I still wear Satan's yoke and love my sins so well."

Rev. John Macleod

When he was about five years old, he enrolled in Fort William public school and remained there until 1885 when he moved on to Aberdeen to continue his education. A booklet called, 'A boyhood in An Gearasdan', which was written by the Principal, gives a fascinating account of his boyhood years in Fort William and introduces us to some of the worthy characters who adorned the town in his day. The booklet appeared in 1992 under the editorship of the Principal's grandson, J. F. M. Macleod of the law firm Macleod and MacCallum, Queensgate, Inverness. It is a welcome contribution to the other writings of Principal John Macleod.

In 1887 when fifteen years old, he entered Aberdeen University and distinguished himself by an academic record which was second to none. In his biography of him, Professor Collins writes: "In 1890, he graduated in Arts, with First Class Honours in Classics, gaining the Simpson Prize in Greek, the Seafield Medal in Latin, the Jenkins Prize in Classical Philology, and the Fullerton Scholarship. His Professor in Latin, Sir William M. Ramsay, and Professor Harrower of the Greek Chair urged him most strongly to take up a Ferguson Classical Scholarship which fell vacant that year, and proceed to Oxford or Cambridge to specialise in Classics. But the young life was already dedicated to higher things; the passion for souls was upon him; and the pleading of his professors was in vain."[37]

John Macleod wanted to be a preacher and a servant of Christ in the church in which he had been baptised, and so he proceeded to prepare himself for that work at the Free Church College in Edinburgh. But those were the days when the Free Church was in turmoil. The Robertson Smith heresy trial had been brought to a conclusion at the Free Church Assembly of 1881, and although the brilliant young Professor was removed from his Chair in Aberdeen, yet his advanced Higher Critical views remained in the Free Church. Later, negotiations for union between the Free and the United Presbyterian Churches were re-opened and to facilitate union and appease the admirers of Robertson Smith, legislation for the introduction of a Declaratory Act was progressed in the Church.

The Declaratory Act was really a conscience clause to circumvent strict adherence to the teaching of the *Westminster Confession of Faith*. The offending Act was eventually adopted by an overwhelming majority in the Free Church but it was claimed to be *ultra-vires* (null and void) by the small group of constitutionalists in the church. At the time John Macleod and some other students signed the following declaration: "A meeting of

---

[37] G. N. M. Collins, *Principal John Macleod*, Edinburgh, 1951, p. 27.

Divinity and Arts Students opposed to the Declaratory Act was held in Glasgow on the evening of Wednesday, November 2nd (1893). The finding of the meeting was as follows: "Seeing the Declaratory Act is now an integral part of the Constitution of the Free Church of Scotland, we the undersigned have ceased to prosecute our studies with a view to the ministry of that church as now constituted." The document was signed by the following divinity students: Allan Mackenzie, James S. Sinclair, Alex Macrae, Neil Cameron, Roderick Mackenzie, and John Macleod. The following Arts students attached their names: George Mackay, Donald Beaton, and Neil MacIntyre. This meant that these young men adhered to the position that was taken by Rev. Donald Macfarlane which brought the Free Presbyterian Church into existence in 1893.

John Macleod had begun his studies for the ministry in New College, Edinburgh, in 1891. But with the passing of Professor George Smeaton two years earlier the spirit of the old Free Church had virtually gone from that noble Theological Institution. Macleod remained in it for only one session and then proceeded to the Irish Presbyterian College in Belfast where he completed his theological Studies. In Belfast he came under the influence of able and Reformed men, one of whom was Professor Robert Watts, a true man of God, for whom he ever afterwards retained the highest affection and regard. Indeed, in later years, books authored by Professor Watts held a foremost place in the Principal's extensive library. Watts had studied at Princeton Theological Seminary and had become an ardent disciple of Professor Charles Hodge. John Macleod became enthusiastic for the Reformed Theology espoused by Hodge and in turn passed that enthusiasm on to the students who passed through his own classes.

After being licensed by the Northern Presbytery of the Free Presbyterian Church, John Macleod was ordained and inducted to the pastoral charge of Lochbroom Free Presbyterian congregation in 1897. In the same year he was also appointed a Theological Tutor for the training of students for the ministry of his Church. The subjects assigned to him were Greek and New Testament Exegesis, and Church History. It was in

Ullapool that he met Margaret Matheson who is described as "a deeply consecrated yoke-fellow, and a woman whose heart had verily felt the touch of God." They were married in April 1898. They had a family of three sons and two daughters. The sons Ian, Alastair, Aeneas, and the daughter Isabel became Medical Practitioners, and Mary, the youngest, became a school teacher.

His ministry in Ullapool was of short duration, and in 1901 he was called to Kames Free Presbyterian congregation. Kames was part of the parish of Kilfinin and embraced Tighnabruaich in Argyllshire. Kames was the first Free Church to declare in favour of the stand taken by the Rev. Donald MacFarlane and Rev. Donald Macdonald over the *Declaratory Act*, and this was due in large measure to the influence of an outstanding and remarkable elder called Archibald Crawford. He was well known among 'the men' of the north, and was a friend and admirer of Dr John Kennedy. His confidence in the 'Constitutionalists' was undermined by the vacillating conduct of one of their leaders – the Rev. Murdoch MacAskill (Dingwall), who, contrary to his protestations against union, ultimately defected to its side. Crawford's support of the stand taken by the Free Presbyterian leaders ensured the success of their cause in the part of Argyll where Crawford was highly respected. John Macleod and he became the best of friends and Macleod tells us that for the last three years of Crawford's life he normally called once or twice a week to see this venerable worthy from whom he learned much. Archibald Crawford died in 1903 and is buried in Kilfinin churchyard. A fascinating and informative account of Archibald Crawford was written by John Macleod and is included as an appendix in Professor Collins' biography of the Principal, which was published in 1951.[38]

After the House of Lords decision in favour of the minority Free Church in 1904, the Church proceeded to repeal all pre-1900 unconstitutional legislation including the Declaratory Act so that the way was now open for re-union with disaffected brethren. This being so, Mr.

[38] As above, pp. 231-285.

Macleod felt it to be a duty to seek clarification of the Free Church's present position regarding her adherence to the *Westminster Confession of Faith* and to that end he moved a motion at the Free Presbyterian Synod held in November 1905. It was to the effect that committees be appointed from both sides to confer on matters of concern and report back to their respective Churches. The motion was defeated by an amendment moved by the Rev. Neil Cameron. Mr Macleod tabled a dissent in the following terms:-

> We, the undersigned ministers and elders of the Synod of the Free Presbyterian Church of Scotland, on our own behalf, and on behalf of as many as adhere to us, dissent from the finding of the Synod anent conference with the Free Church, inasmuch as by refusing even to hold a conference, a policy of disunion and division is being pursued, and what does not justify the making of a separation does not justify the maintaining of it; and, moreover, we feel ourselves at liberty, either jointly or individually, to do whatever we can by conference to heal the breach between the two branches of the Free Church of Scotland adhering to its Disruption position."

This dissent was signed by "John Macleod, George Mackay, Alexander Stewart (ministers) and Hugh Thomson (elder)."

The dissenting ministers met with representatives from the Free Church and having been satisfied as to the Free Church's return to the basic principles of the Disruption they were admitted to the Free Church by a special meeting of Commission of Assembly in December, 1905. Rev. Alexander Stewart carried most of his congregation with him and retained their place of worship in East Fountainbridge. The Rev. George Mackay was called to the vacant Free Church congregation of Stornoway. A Free Presbyterian student, Mr James Sinclair, on completing his theological course, was ordained and inducted to Latheron Free Church. Rev. John Macleod was elected and appointed to the Chair of Greek and New Testament Exegesis by the General Assembly of 1906. His inaugural

71

address, which was delivered in the Free Church College on 18th October, 1906, was separately printed for distribution.[39]

John Macleod would have graced any Chair in the Free Church College but he was undoubtedly suited to the Greek one, and his distinguished University record in Greek, Latin, and Philology qualified him for the department of New Testament. Dr Alexander Ross, who at a later date occupied the same Chair, was one of Professor Macleod's students and he had this to say of his old teacher: "Professor Macleod's complete mastery of the Greek language was patent to all his students, some of whom, of course, were far from experiencing the enthusiasm for that ancient tongue which possessed him." He went on to say: "I recall some fine exegetical notes which he gave us on the Epistle to the Romans, which helped us to attain to a deeper insight into some of the great passages in that profound Epistle, which Samuel Taylor Coleridge, I think, described as the greatest piece of writing in the world. The theology of that Epistle was expounded to us in all its majesty and depth and fullness, for the Professor was a widely-read and well-informed theologian, as well as a careful and accurate Greek exegete."[40]

There were many, both within and outwith the Free Church, who believed that Professor Macleod was in the place where he would be able to exercise a profound influence upon the theological scene. His unashamed love of Calvinistic doctrine would win for it the respect it deserved. He would enhance the Free Church College's reputation as a bastion of Reformed Orthodoxy. It was therefore a great disappointment to many when as we have seen the Church in its wisdom translated him to the charge in Inverness.

On the 23rd of July, 1913, Professor Macleod was inducted to the Free North Church and was given a warm welcome to the Highland capital. The reception was presided over by Rev. Donald Maclean who was later

---

[39] The lecture was entitled 'The Place of New Testament Exegesis in Theological Study.' It was printed for private circulation (Glasgow, 1907).
[40] Collins, *John Macleod*, p 105.

to be one of his colleagues in the Free Church College. And so began a ministry of seventeen years.

Times were changing and all too soon Dr Macleod was aware that the serene and leisurely Edwardian age was disappearing and being replaced by dark and sinister days. War clouds gathered over Europe and within months of the new minister's arrival in Inverness the country was plunged into a bitter and bloody conflict that would end with the loss of nearly 900,000 British service men and women, along with a similar number who would be permanently injured and mentally scarred by their experiences. In one way or another, the war affected all the churches. Young men were called to volunteer for the armed services and when massive numbers of reinforcements were required conscription was introduced. The Free North Church suffered like others as young men had to leave their homes. During the war the hall was taken over by the military for the billeting of troops and this meant the curtailment of some congregational activities. The church never forgot her young men and they never forgot their church. War comforts, as they were called, consisting of knitted woollen scarves, gloves, and socks, were sent to the boys who in turn sent back cards of appreciation. The burden of prayer during those years was for the cessation of hostilities and a return to peace.

In the Spring of 1918, when the last great German offensive took place at Amiens, the British line was broken and French troops retreated. It was a blow to the allied cause for it meant that the German strategy to divide the allied forces and put the channel ports at risk was succeeding. The offensive failed. The German army was pushed back and cleared from western Belgium and Northern France and an armistice was agreed on 11th November, 1918.

In the Free North Kirk Session minute for the 5th of December, 1918, the following is recorded. "The Session desire to put on record the fact that the congregation held a special prayer meeting at 8 p.m. almost every evening without a break from March the twenty fourth until the fifth day of December. This meeting was held for the special purpose of interceding with God on behalf of our country and our country's cause in connection with the Great War, and also for the purpose of seeking a revival of true religion. It began when the serious German offensive started, and was kept until the evening when the special service of thanksgiving was held which was appointed by the Commission of General Assembly on the cessation of hostilities. From the day when the Armistice was signed, namely the eleventh of November, the meeting took the special form of thanksgiving for victory vouchsafed, and the Session desire to record their gratitude to the Lord for enabling so many of the congregation evening after evening to continue instant in prayer during trying and anxious months and for the issue to which the dreadful war has come which lasted from the fourth day of August, 1914, until the eleventh day of November, 1918. At the same time, they record the fact that about ninety young men of families connected with the congregation laid down their lives for their country in these sad but eventful years, and they express their sympathy with the many homes that have been thus shadowed with sorrow."

In one way or another the war had an effect upon the religious life of the nation and along with other congregations the Free North also suffered. Young men who would otherwise have married and had families to bring to the church of their fathers never returned from war service and now they lie forgotten in some corner of a foreign field. There were others who survived but they preferred to settle elsewhere rather than return to the town of their birth. While some of those who did come home had become used to a way of life in which God was dishonoured, His Word neglected, His Day set aside, and His Church had become an irrelevancy.

The Free North pastorate entailed the spiritual oversight of a considerable congregation which was no easy task. Indeed, to succeed Murdo Mackenzie was daunting enough. Mackenzie had outstanding gifts as a preacher. His powerful voice reached the furthest corners of the massive church building. There was also passion and verve in Mackenzie's style, and in his eloquent delivery he could raise his audience with him to great heights of heavenly thought, or reduce them to tears of penitence according to the theme of his sermon. He was also an excellent administrator in church affairs and was a born leader of men. Macleod, on the other hand, had great reasoning powers and a tremendous memory so that he could recall from a well stored mind what was apposite to his theme. In his biography we are told that "His voice had a fine carrying range without being strident." His words were well chosen and his exegesis of Scripture was always truly biblical. We are informed that "His pulpit mannerisms were few, but they were peculiarly his own. When he was in happy frame, he used to rock backwards and forwards on his feet with his thumbs inserted in the upper pockets of his waistcoat, while the sermon flowed in spate."[41] Macleod too was an excellent church administrator and a born leader. Professor Collins recalls the verdict of one of the summer student assistants who writes of summer days in the nineteen twenties. "The Free North of those days was a model congregation. Organisation could hardly be improved upon; attendances were excellent and the loyalty of the people was manifested in their hearty support of all the schemes of the Church. The Kirk Session was representative of some of the leading business concerns in the town as well as of the humbler occupations. Fortunate indeed was the congregation which was served by such men as John Campbell, Roderick Macleod, Donald Campbell, James Gordon, Alexander Fraser, John Cameron, Donald MacLennan, Donald Maclean, John MacPherson, Duncan Mackay and Donald Mackenzie – to mention but some of them – with, to quote the Principal's own description of him, 'the shrewd, eagle-eyed John Fraser' as Session Clerk. Under the competent leadership of William Simpson, at the English services, and Alexander Fraser ('Sandy the coachbuilder') at the Gaelic, the congregational praise was something to remember; and to be waited upon in vestry and pulpit by warm-hearted Peter Mackenzie was to be served by the ideal Church Officer."

It was a mammoth task to visit each home in the congregation and in later years owing to illness he was only able to visit the sick and the elderly. His visits were welcome and he would often surprise parents by quoting the exact date of a child's birth or baptism from his amazing memory. To

---

[41] Collins, *John Macleod*, p.73

quote from his biography, "In conversation with his people he exercised the most scrupulous care. He loved to hear, and tell, a good story, but he avoided levity. Gossip and small talk were to him abhorrent. If anyone should venture on those lines he would soon learn his mistake. 'Quite so,' the Principal would ejaculate disarmingly, and then he would adroitly switch the conversation on to other topics."[42]

In 1920 he was appointed Moderator of the Free Church General Assembly. His opening address to the Assembly was, 'The Outlook in Regard to the Maintenance of the Reformed Faith.' In the course of his remarks on the importance of creedal subscription, he said among other things, "Men deceive themselves when they think that by jettisoning the ship's cargo and lightening her of her load of Christian dogma she will ride the storm better and come safely into harbour. The inevitable end of the present trend of things is just such a wretched patchwork of negations and bloodless morality as has formed the staple of unevangelical pulpit work in every age. The hungry sheep look up and are not fed, the drawing power of the Cross being wanting. The outcome of this state of things has been and will be empty pews and a paganised population." Emphasising the need for the Free Church to maintain the historic faith of the past, he said: "Holding to the historic faith and worship of Scotland's Reformed Church, she is content in a day of reproach to share the reproach of a despised Evangel, and look for her vindication not only to the day when the Church's reproach shall be forever removed; she also cherishes the hope that with a gracious revival of true godliness the people of the land of covenants and martyrs will yet retrace the steps by which they strayed from the good way, and that will be a vindication of her contendings."[43]

His ability was recognised beyond his own Church and being keenly interested in Scottish Education he was for several years Chairman of the old Inverness-shire Education Authority. We are told that at meetings, "he was always equable and fair, and while he was obviously most

---

[42] As above, pp. 143-4.
[43] As above, p. 122.

knowledgeable, he was at the same time sparing in utterance." Mr. Murdo Morrison, who was then Director of Education, writes: "he was unremittingly attentive and suggestive at every point in the discussion and exercised a minimum of interference as long as members kept to the subject before them. Though he was essentially modest, it was not safe to take undue liberties with him in the Chair."[44]

Another interest of his was the evangelical traditions of the Highlands and of Gaeldom's contribution to the Gaelic religious ethos. In 1927 when invited by the Gaelic Society of Inverness to address them, he did so on the subject, 'The North Country Separatists.' It was printed and produced in 1930, and reproduced in 1965 with the excision of the parts written in Gaelic in *By-paths of Highland Church History*. It is a most informative contribution on the subject of 'Separatism' in the Church in the Highlands.

In 1926 his health began to suffer under the strain of his many duties. Not only had he the oversight of a large congregation, but he was frequently engaged at communion services throughout the church. He also served on the Church's Standing Committees and generally as a convener. Few realise how demanding committee work can be and the responsibility that rests upon the convener. In order to have some respite he was given leave of absence from his pulpit and was able to fulfil a lifelong desire to visit the Holy Land. He and his wife left by steamer on 9th April, 1926, and sailed to Port Said. After some sightseeing, they moved on to Cairo where they visited Tutankhamen's tomb, the Pyramids, and journeyed along the banks of the Nile. From Cairo they crossed the Suez Canal and on to Jerusalem and visited the Biblical sights which they wished to see. They arrived home early in May.

The following year was a memorable one for him. The University of Aberdeen, where he had distinguished himself as a brilliant student, conferred upon him the honorary degree of Doctor of Divinity. In that same year, following the death of Dr J. D. MacCulloch, he was the unanimous choice of the 1927 General Assembly to succeed him as

---

[44] As above, p. 115.

Principal of the College. In October, Dr Macleod was inducted to his office and on the 19th of that month he gave his inaugural lecture on the subject, 'Our Work as a Theological College,' in which "he pledged the College to fidelity to the Reformed system of doctrine." Under his wise and strong leadership there was to be no compromise with what was in opposition to the gospel. He emphasised the trustworthiness of the New Testament and said, "Behind the witness of the Apostles we cannot make our way. Beyond the teaching of the Apostles we cannot go. To be loyal to them and to their Lord means that we brush aside as so many impertinences the protean forms in which Modernism would neutralise this authority. The issue is between the historic faith of Evangelical Christendom and another religion altogether. There is but one gospel, and another Gospel is a rival to it. It is something different from the gospel entirely. It is vain to make room in the Christian nest for the alien intruder, and at the same time to think that the legitimate and natural inmates of that nest shall be left safe in their own home. Admit the alien, make room for the intruder, and you doom the home born to extrusion and to banishment. Or, if they are suffered to remain they do so as helots that minister to the caprice of the domineering intruder."[45]

Although he was now Principal of the College, he also continued in the pastorate of the Free North Church. It was hoped that he would soon recover his health and strength for these demanding tasks and it seemed to be so when once more he gave himself to his work with enthusiasm. In 1927, however, he had a severe attack of bronchial trouble with overstrain of the heart, and his medical adviser recommended a prolonged period of convalescence and a change to a warmer climate. A free-will offering was made by the congregation, and in the Spring of 1928, when he had sufficiently recovered, he and his wife sailed for Australia where brethren from our sister church there extended to him a warm invitation to be their guest. They left on 10th February, 1928, and disembarked at Sydney on

---

[45] As above, pp. 130-1.

22nd March. On 26th July, they returned home, via New Zealand, Canada, and America.

Dr Macleod's ministry in Inverness was soon to end. In August, 1929, Professor W. Menzies Alexander, who occupied the Chair of Apologetics, Natural Science, Homiletics, and Pastoral Theology, died. In his book *Annals of the Free Church of Scotland 1900-86*, Professor Collins gives us some interesting information about Alexander's background. "Dr Alexander was of Covenanter stock, and several of his forebears had been active on the side of the persecuted Hillmen. His mother was a Menzies, and an ancestress of hers, Lucy Menzies, had the sad distinction of befriending the young widow of John Brown, of Priesthill, and her children, on the day in 1685 that her godly husband was shot dead before her eyes by Claverhouse and his dragoons."[46]

Alexander was a distinguished student and a man of outstanding ability. He had the distinction of being the holder of Doctorates in Medicine, Science, and Divinity. He was ordained in 1889 and began his ministry on the academic side of missionary work in Bombay in India. After some years on the mission field he returned home. In 1902 he published a book *Demonic Possession in the New Testament*, which gained for him a certain notoriety for what were considered to be advanced critical views. When he realised the furore it caused in certain quarters, he recalled the book at great cost to himself with the result that it is now a very rare volume.[47] He was admitted from the United Free Church in 1904, and was appointed to the Chair of Apologetics. "He rendered great service in the re-organisation of the Free Church College after 1900 – and he carried through the daunting work of reconstruction which was completed by a fully manned Senate in 1905."[48] In his day Dr Alexander was an ornament of the Free Church and distinguished himself as a teacher of students until

---

[46] G N. M. Collins (compiler), *Annals of the Free Church of Scotland 1900-1986*, Edinburgh, 1987, p. 6.
[47] This book was reprinted by Baker Book House, Grand Rapids, Michigan, in 1980, and by digital print-to-order publishers in more recent years.
[48] Collins, *Annals*, p.6.

his death in 1929. He was a man of God who was committed to the Free Church in her adherence to the Reformed Faith, as expressed in the *Westminster Confession of Faith*.

There was only one man who could replace Professor Alexander, and that was John Macleod. It was the Rev. Norman Campbell of Dingwall at the 1930 Assembly who proposed Dr Macleod's name. Dr Macleod, he said, had all the knowledge necessary for this Chair, but scholarship was not everything. He was inclined to think he could trace the decline of the old Free Church to the fact that there came a time when more regard was paid to scholarship than to piety. Students became scholars and were not influenced by piety in their teachers. They had in their Church a scholar who was a man of great weight of character as well as piety. He was also a man of wisdom and tact, and he knew of no one to whom he would entrust the education of young men preparing for the ministry more confidently than Dr Macleod.

It wasn't easy for the Free North to part with their minister, nor was it easy for the Principal to part with his people. The bond between them throughout his seventeen years of ministry had remained "strong and unstrained." He bowed, however, to the will of the Church, and on 29th July, 1930, he was inducted to his College Chair. He gave his inaugural lecture on the 15th of October on the subject, 'The Place of Apologetics in a Theological Curriculum.' As expected, Dr Macleod gave his undivided attention to the work of preparing men for the ministry, and being a scholar of rare attainments, he passed on to them the wealth of a well stored mind, as well as the wealth of years of experience in pastoral ministry. Even more important to them was how he impressed them with a sense of the dignity and godliness so becoming for a Christian. It was something that they never forgot. We are told by his biographer that his classroom prayers, "were an unconscious unveiling of his own devout soul, and frequently had the effect of transforming the classroom into a sanctuary where God seemed wondrously near."[49]

---

[49] Collins, *John Macleod*, p.151-2.

In 1932, his like-minded wife passed on to be with Christ and this left a great blank in his life. She was buried in the Grange Cemetery in Edinburgh, in a spot not far from the corner where the mortal remains of some of the brightest stars of the old Free Church lie buried awaiting the glorious day of the resurrection.

This is recorded in the *Minute* of 17th May, 1932, concerning the passing of Principal Macleod's wife: "The Kirk Session of the Free North Church congregation, Inverness, being specially convened, learn with regret of the passing of Mrs. Macleod, the wife of Principal Macleod, their late pastor. They remember with gratitude her devoted service in connection with the various activities of the congregation, during the able pastorate of her distinguished husband. They convey to the Principal and his family their profound sympathy, and pray that in this their hour of great sorrow, the God of all grace may be their Comforter and Sustainer." Two of the Session were appointed to attend the funeral in Edinburgh, and hand to the Principal an excerpt of the Minute. The Principal responded by a letter written in June, in which he thanked the Session on his own and on his family's behalf for this expression of sympathy. He added: "my dear wife loved the congregation and spared no effort, within the compass of her power to further its highest welfare. Convey my greeting to the brethren." A stone marks the spot with the simple words inscribed, 'Called and Kept.' And now his own body rests there too.

His home at Rillbank Terrace became a place where many of the leading Reformed Theologians of the day were made welcome. Professor J. Gresham Machen who with likeminded colleagues established Westminster Theological Seminary and made it a bastion of Reformed Orthodoxy, visited him in 1932. Principal Macleod welcomed this doughty defender of the Faith as a fellow combatant in the cause of Biblical Truth. When the old-style Calvinism of Princeton was being weakened in the 1920s, by a policy of accommodation towards Liberalism, Principal Macleod's sympathies were with Machen, Robert Dick Wilson, O. T. Allis, and their colleagues, whom he regarded as the true successors of Princeton's giants of the past. In support of Westminster, we are informed that, "he enriched their library with considerable consignments of theological treasures from his own well-furnished shelves."

In 1937 a special lectureship was set up in the Free Church College which resulted in some of the finest exponents of Reformed Doctrine visiting Edinburgh. The lectureship made an impact upon all who were in sympathy with conservative theology. The first lecturer was Professor Oswald T. Allis of Westminster Seminary. In 1938, Professor William Childs Robinson of Columbia Theological Seminary, Decatur, U.S.A. delivered a series under the title, 'The Word of the Cross.' The lectures were published in book form by the Sovereign Grace Union. In 1939 Professor Auguste Lecerf, of the Protestant Faculty of Theology in the University of Paris, who was described as "the erudite leader of revived Calvinism in John Calvin's native land," was lecturer. In 1941 Dr Martyn Lloyd-Jones delivered lectures which were published under the title, *The Plight of Man and the Power of God.*[50] Others who visited the Principal prior to 1939 were Professor Cornelius Van Til of Westminster and Professor John Murray of the same seminary. John Murray and John Macleod were close friends and whenever in the homeland, Murray would visit his friend.

There were two occasions in the 1930s when the Principal was required to cross the Atlantic. The first was in 1935. A colonial branch of the Church of Scotland in Prince Edward Island, which was in close agreement with the Free Church in doctrine, desired closer links with the Free Church. In response to their petition the Principal and the Rev. Norman Campbell of Dingwall were appointed deputies to visit the Island and confer with brethren there. The deputies discharged their duties and at the same time they visited some of the Free Church congregations in Canada. On their return they reported their findings to the Church at home.

The second occasion when Dr Macleod visited America was in 1939 prior to the outbreak of the second world war. In 1939 Westminster Theological Seminary in Philadelphia secured its charter for awarding

---

[50] Published by Pickering and Inglis in 1942, and reprinted many times since then.

degrees and it was decided by the faculty that it should celebrate this and its tenth anniversary by inviting a distinguished theologian of the Reformed School to deliver special lectures. Principal Macleod was their choice and his subject was 'Scottish Theology in Relation to Church History Since the Reformation.' He accepted the invitation and sailed for New York on 17th March, 1939, accompanied by his daughter, Dr Isabel Macleod. They arrived at their destination on 27th March. There were ten lectures, and the first was delivered on the 3rd April. The lectures were well received by an appreciative audience and the desire was repeatedly expressed that the lectures be made available to the public in book form so that they could be studied at leisure. The outbreak of war in September 1939 hindered immediate publication, but eventually the Free Church Publications Committee released the first edition in 1943. A second edition was called for in 1946. Since then, it has been reprinted in conjunction with the Banner of Truth Trust.

Principal Macleod at Westminster Theological Seminary in 1939.

It is a superb piece of work and it gives a clear picture of the various theological trends in the story of the Scottish Kirk. It is a book that should be read and re-read. It is worth its weight in gold. Professor G. T. Thomson, of the Chair of Dogmatics in Edinburgh New College, wrote of it: "Northing known to us covers this field like *Scottish Theology*. Yet the finest detail obviously proceeds, not from painful *ad hoc* labours, but from a well-stocked memory, here committed direct to paper from the pen of a ready writer. Just as from his armchair in his own study surrounded by his own treasure trove in the realms of theological history he expounds to the eager listener the human side and the living passion of Scotland's struggles towards freedom, so here he communicates almost orally to paper and print the national progress through suffering to a triumph of Reformed unity, perhaps today fragmented yet still a burning hope to many of us, pointing to a still loftier goal of achievement for human kind. It makes one tremble to think that, being so familiar with all that he relates, Dr Macleod might not have considered recording it for posterity."[51]

Principal Macleod carried out a number of engagements after delivering his lectures and on the 18th of August he returned home on board the *S.S. Athenia*. It was to be *Athenia's* last crossing of the Atlantic. On September 4th, 1939, she was reported to have been torpedoed by a German U-Boat about 200 miles west of the Hebrides on her way to Canada. This was in contravention of the Prize Laws which Germany had signed in 1936 which made it illegal to sink a ship without securing the safety of her passengers. 18 persons lost their lives, they were among the first casualties of the Battle of the Atlantic.

It had been hoped that Principal Macleod would have authored a great deal more than he did, but he was a modest man who complained of a lazy pen and so a great deal of his material is fugitive. In 1929 Dr John R. Mackay, the Professor of Greek in the Free Church College, in consultation with Professors Maclean and Macleod decided to launch a new theological review to replace in some measure *The Princeton Theological Review*, which had ceased publication. Dr Mackay and Dr Maclean became joint editors of the new magazine, which was called *The Evangelical Quarterly*. Principal Macleod became a consulting editor and remained so until his death, and he also contributed some articles to the publication. It was a highly successful journal, and remained so until after Professor Maclean's death in 1942. It to this day contains some sound articles written by the leading scholars and theologians and historians of the day.

In 1930, Principal Macleod produced his booklet on *The North Country Separatists*. In 1932 he edited a new edition of Dr Kennedy's life of *The Apostle of the North* and in that volume the Principal included his English translation of the Apostle's Gaelic poem on 'The Christian on His Way to

---

[51] Collins, *John Macleod*, p. 182.

Jordan,' on 'Jordan's Banks,' and 'Beyond the Jordan.' In 1939 he edited a memorial volume of Dr Donald Munro in which he wrote a sketch of his friend's life. In the early 1940s he wrote a Foreword to Dr Alexander Stewart's book, *Shoes for the Road*. As we have seen, in 1943 his *magnum opus* – *Scottish Theology* – appeared. His biography, written by Professor Collins, was published in 1951. An Appendix contains two biographical sketches by the Principal, one on Finlay Munro, 'A Highland Evangelist,' and the other on Archibald Crawford, 'An Argyllshire Worthy.' His book, *By-paths of Highland Church History*, was edited and produced by Professor Collins in 1965. *Some Favourite Books*, being articles written for *The Monthly Record* between 1918 and 1922, was printed by the Banner of Truth Trust in 1988. *A Boyhood in An Gearasden* was reprinted from Volume LVII of the *Transactions of the Gaelic Society of Inverness* by the Principal's grandson J. F. M. Macleod, M.A., LLB.

In 1942 John Macleod retired from his offices as Principal and Professor. At the 1942 Assembly he was presented with an illuminated address, a cheque, and arrangements were made to have a portrait done of him by the artist David Foggie. It is now displayed in the College. He reached his jubilee in the ministry in 1947, and on 11th July, 1948, he peacefully left this world to be with Christ, which is far better. His mortal remains are buried alongside his wife's in the Grange cemetery in Edinburgh.

Principal John Macleod was an outstanding scholar, theologian, and churchman, but more than that, he was a humble, gracious, and devout servant of God. His biographer tells us that, "At the end of the Session he delivered his closing address in obvious weakness, and, indeed, distress. His farewell words were deeply moving. Looking back over the years of his teaching service in the College, he expressed the fear that perhaps unknowingly, he had grieved or wronged some who had passed through his hands, adding, 'If that should be the case, I beg their forgiveness, as I seek forgiveness of my God.'"[52] John Macleod gave strong leadership to

---

[52] Collins, *John Macleod*, p. 188-9.

the Free Church of Scotland in his day, he was a faithful preacher of the gospel, and he made the Free Church College a highly respected institution of Reformed scholarship.

CHAPTER 5

KENNETH CAMERON

IN 1930 a vacancy committee was appointed by the Free North congregation under the chairmanship of the Rev. Alexander Macleod of Croy who had been appointed interim-moderator of the congregation. At a meeting held on Monday 15th September, 1930, Mr John Fraser, the Session Clerk intimated that the name that commended itself unanimously to the committee was that of the Rev. Kenneth Cameron, the Minister of Stornoway Free Church. It was stated in the vacancy committee minute that, "Mr. Cameron's many good qualities, – his outstanding ability as a preacher, – the favourable impression created amongst the members of the congregation through personal intercourse with that gentleman from time to time and the interesting fact of his previous close association with the Free North Church in his earlier days" had weighed with them in their choice. Steps were now taken to present him with a call and on 23rd October 1930 about 1,000 people attached their names to it. The call was tabled and disposed of at the Lewis Presbytery on 13th November, when Mr Cameron intimated his acceptance.

Kenneth Cameron was born on 9th August, 1876, at 6 Fraser Street, The Haugh, Inverness. His father was a railwayman who belonged to the town, and his mother was Ann Fraser who hailed from Croy. They were Free Church people and attended the Free North in the days when Dr

George Mackay was minister and when the congregation worshipped in the old building on North Lane. Kenneth their son has recorded the fact that his father was baptised by Dr Mackay and that in his youth he sat under Murdo Mackenzie's ministry, so that he was no stranger to the congregation which now called him to be their pastor.

He had a distinguished record as a scholar. He attended Raining School, Inverness, where for two successive years he was First Prizeman. After schooldays he proceeded to Edinburgh University where he was a keen and diligent student. He was a prizeman in Celtic Literature, and took high places in English Literature, Latin and Greek. It must have been in his teenage years that he experienced the saving grace of God, for on completion of university studies he decided to serve the Lord in the ministry of the gospel. After graduation he proceeded to New College, Edinburgh, once the bastion of Reformed Orthodoxy, but now no longer so. Here he remained for two years. His teachers were Principal Robert Rainy – Church History; Professor A. B. Davidson – Hebrew and Old Testament; Marcus Dods – Greek and New Testament; John Laidlaw – Systematic Theology; and Alexander Martin – Apologetics. In New College he showed proficiency, especially in New Testament Greek and Old Testament Language and Literature. After the crisis of 1900 he was one of the few students to identify with the minority who continued the Free Church and he did so at some cost to himself, for he forfeited a substantial bursary on which he was largely dependent. He pursued his divinity studies at Edinburgh University and while there was prizeman in Ecclesiastical History. He spent a further session in the Divinity Hall of the United Original Secession Church.

I have been informed by his grandson, Kenneth, that his grandfather did a summer assistantship with G. H. Morrison in Thurso in 1898. Dr G. H. Morrison, as he later became, was an able and gifted student in the pre-1900 Free Church. In 1893 he was invited to become assistant to the famous Dr Alexander Whyte of the premier Free Church charge of St George's in Edinburgh. Although there were inducements for Morrison to remain in Edinburgh, he was prevailed upon in 1894 to move north to

Thurso to become colleague and successor to Dr Walter Ross Taylor who had been minister in the town since before the Disruption in 1843. Ross Taylor was a conservative evangelical who had served his day well but had now reached the stage when it was necessary to pass the burden on to a younger man. Taylor died in 1896 at the advanced age of 91. Morrison was at the commencement of his ministry and was beginning to develop pulpit gifts which were to take him far.

In 1898 Morrison was translated to St John's Free Church in Dundee. He was not to remain there for long, for in 1902 he was called to the Wellington United Free Church in University Avenue, Glasgow, where he was to remain for the rest of his days until his sudden death in 1928 when only 62 years old. He was a popular preacher, and his Sunday evening services drew capacity crowds. Long queues formed in University Avenue before the Church doors were opened and this continued throughout Morrison's ministry. His style of preaching, which was popular rather than theological, can be gauged from the numerous books of sermons which flowed from his pen. They can provide seed thoughts for young preachers even today. Among these volumes are, *Sun-Rise, Flood-Tide, Unlighted Lustre, The Wings of the Morning*, and others.

In his early years, when minister in Dundee, Morrison also brought out a new edition of Thomas Boston's *Memoirs* in which he included an introduction and notes. It was published in 1899. Kenneth Cameron could not but learn from this young, enthusiastic and hardworking minister and that was seen later in his own pulpit style and in his own unflagging zeal in His Master's service.

In 1902 Mr Cameron was ordained and inducted to Clyne Free Church where he remained for seven years. In 1906 he married Annie Cameron who came from Garve in Ross-shire. Her father was a forester there who also worked on the railway. On 29th November, 1907, their son, William John, was born. He was to distinguish himself as a minister of the Free Church. After pastorates in Burghead, in Morayshire, and Buccleuch and Greyfriars, in Edinburgh, he was appointed in 1953, Professor of Greek and New Testament in the Free Church College. He became

Principal in 1973 and retired in 1977. He was twice appointed Moderator of Assembly, first in 1962 and again in 1977. Incidentally, William John's son, named Kenneth after his grandfather, became Free Church minister in Prince Edward Island, Coatbridge, Thurso, was missionary-minister in Umtata, South Africa, and is now retired. He was Moderator of the Free Church in 1989.

In 1909 the Duirinish congregation in Skye addressed a call to Mr. Cameron which he accepted. It was a congregation that had known revival under the ministry of Alexander M'Coll who laboured there from 1852-70, and it had enjoyed spiritual enrichment under his successor, the Rev. John M'Rae. In those days Gaelic was the native language in Skye and the new minister, although a Gaelic scholar, was soon at home speaking in the colloquial language of the people and he was equally versatile in preaching in Gaelic in its biblical form each Lord's Day.

He was very happy among the Duirinish people and they were fond of their active young pastor. In an article that appeared in the *Monthly Record* in 1947, from the pen of Rev. Kenneth MacRae, we are informed that Mr Cameron "ever cherished a warm spot in his heart for Skye and its religious associations." It was in Duirinish that his daughter Annie was born. She brought great happiness to the manse, but it was only to be for a short time.

The large and influential congregation in Stornoway in Lewis was to be his next sphere of service. Their minister in 1900 was Peter Macdonald who entered the United Free Church at the time of the union. He was succeeded in 1906 by Rev. George Mackay who had been admitted from the Free Presbyterian Church in 1904. His ministry was from 1906 to 1910 when he was translated to Fearn. The Stornoway people now set their hearts on securing the young energetic minister of Duirinish whom they felt would be a suitable pastor for them in every way. He, however, did not see it as his duty to go there and declined their invitation. But when they approached him a second time they were successful and on the 19th of August, 1914, he was inducted to the congregation of Stornoway, where he was to remain until 1930.

When Mr. Cameron arrived in Stornoway the country was about to be plunged into a war that was to last for four weary and bitter years and leave many homes in Stornoway and throughout the island devastated by the tragic loss of young life. The ministerial visits to bereaved households were never easy, rather they were extremely stressful especially if more than one son from a family was killed by enemy action or lost at sea. There was also the appalling loss of life in 1919 when the *Iolaire* sank as she was approaching Stornoway harbour. Young men returning home from war service were waiting for transport at Kyle of Lochalsh. The *Iolaire* was sent to take them to their island home. Families were waiting with joyful anticipation for the reunion that was to mark the beginning of a New Year and a new era of peace. It was not to be: the *Iolaire* foundered within a short distance of the harbour with large loss of life. Bodies were brought to Stornoway for identification, and then taken to their respective homes for burial. The tragedy cast a gloom over Stornoway town and the congregation on Kenneth Street felt it. Mr Cameron's own home was left grief stricken when their little girl was removed from them by death when she was only five years old. He knew what sorrow was and how to comfort those in similar distress.

As well as attending to his pastoral duties in Stornoway he was frequently a member of the Standing Committees of the Church and invariably was convener of one or other of them. Another matter that took up his time was serving as an active member of the School Board, and Education Authorities' Committees in Sutherland, Ross & Cromarty, and Inverness, which he did for over a period of twenty-five years. He was, along with the Rev. John Macdonald of Rosskeen, a delegate to the meeting of the Pan-Presbyterian Alliance which was held at Pittsburgh, U.S.A., in 1921, and, along with Dr A. M. Renwick and Rev. John MacDonald, Glasgow, he was sent out to Vancouver in 1923. In 1924 he was Moderator of the General Assembly of the Free Church.

Mr Cameron's induction to the Free North took place on 23rd December, 1930, with a Presbytery lunch in the Queensgate Hotel, presided over by Professor Donald Maclean, and a congregational

Rev. Kenneth Cameron

gathering in the Church in the evening at 8 o'clock, with the Rev. A. Macleod, Croy, as Chairman. When the Kirk Session met in January, 1931, a cordial welcome was extended to the new minister expressing the desire that "he would be spared long to carry on the Lord's work in the congregation, and that his labours would be blessed richly." He responded by thanking them for their welcome and saying, "that he would do all in his power to further the spiritual interests of the congregation. He was sure that there would be mutual co-operation towards this end." And so, a new era in the congregation's history began.

The congregation in the 1930s had declined in numbers since the great days of Murdo Mackenzie whose charismatic presence had made a tremendous impact on the Highlands so that, when the majority of Free Church people moved into the new United Free Church, those who sided with Mackenzie never left him. However, the unkind and unchristian propaganda emanating from both the press and the new United Free Church could not but have an effect. The Free Church was vilified and cast in the mould of being a rogue Church whose only interest was in the spoils that followed and to which they were legally entitled by the judgement of the House of Lords. The Church was also decried as being purely Highland and lacking in men of intellectual stature. And so, it was derided and dubbed, the 'Wee Frees.' Such persistent criticism established a prejudice against the Free Church with the result that it was to some extent marginalised especially in the south of Scotland. The devastating effects of the First World War also took its toll as did the spirit of the age. For example, attitudes were changing and the roaring twenties was dominated by the flamboyant and hedonistic carefree lifestyles of the new, flapper age, as it was called. Everyday life was also being influenced by the attractions of the Hollywood silver screen. Against this background the Church had to fight for her voice to be heard.

In Inverness the new Free Church minister set about getting to know his congregation, and he did this by a process of systematic visitation. He did not have a car but the town was very much smaller than it is today and so week by week he walked the streets of Inverness to call on the homes of his people. If necessary, he would hire a taxi to take him to those who were some distance away. We do not know how long it took him to cover the town but it was a tiring task and one that he repeated continually until his ministry ended with his retirement. His visits were never prolonged affairs. If his knock was not responded to almost immediately then he left for the next home. When admitted it was to wait for a short time, ask how everyone was, and then commit them all to God in prayer.

He was a scholarly man who prepared carefully and prayerfully for the pulpit. His preaching was concise and to the point, and he never wearied his audience. Any guest preacher invited to his pulpit was reminded of when the service should end, and he would express disapproval if the guest preacher ventured beyond his time. An appreciation of Mr Cameron appeared in the 'Current Topics' column of the *Monthly Record* of August 1947. It describes him as "an able preacher of the Evangel, who put to good use the brilliant talents with which he had been endowed." It goes on to say: "The present writer remembers well a sermon preached by him in Dingwall in 1903, on the Fast Day of a Communion Season, on the words in the 51st Psalm, 'Create in me a clean heart, O God.' That sermon was full of sound and well-ordered theology, yet there was nothing dull or heavy about it, for it was characterised by an attractive freshness of presentation and it was delivered with much vigour, while the wooing note of winsome appeal could be clearly heard from time to time in it."

A good specimen of his type and style of preaching can be read in a book of sermons published in 1927 called, *The Free Church Pulpit*. The text is, "And when they were come to the place, which is called Calvary, there they crucified Him" (Luke 23:33). The sermon is called 'Calvary,' and he brings out the following points: Calvary – the place of Suffering; Calvary – the place of Revelation; Calvary – the place of Victory; Calvary – the place of Blessing; and Calvary – the place of Condemnation. It is typical of his concise, well-ordered, presentation of the gospel.[53]

Sabbath was always a busy day. Since its formation the North Church was the main Gaelic Church in the town and down the years the Gaelic service was held at 11 am. in the Church, an English service was held at 2 pm in the afternoon, the Sabbath School met at 5 o'clock, and two evening services were held at 6.30 pm, one in English in the Church, and the other in Gaelic in the hall. The evening Gaelic service was generally conducted by a Gaelic speaking office-bearer. As Gaelic ceased to be the spoken language in these parts and Gaelic attendances began to diminish, change had to come. In 1933, it was decided to hold the English service in the Church at 11am, followed immediately afterwards by a Gaelic service. The Sunday School was to meet at 12 noon in the hall. The afternoon English service at 2pm ceased. The two evening services carried on as before.

There were two events of special significance celebrated in the 1930s when special services were held in the Church to commemorate them. One was the silver jubilee of King George V[th] and Queen Mary on 6th May, 1935, and the other was the coronation of King George VIth and Queen Elizabeth in May 1937.

Another special event bearing upon the congregation was the celebration of its centenary when special services of thanksgiving were held to commemorate the commencement of the congregation on 15th January 1837. Services were conducted by Mr Cameron the minister and Principal John Macleod the former pastor. There were large and appreciative gatherings at the services to thank God for the past and to look forward to the future with courage. A communication was received from the Presbytery of Inverness and was included in the minutes of the Kirk Session. It reads:

---

[53] *The Free Church Pulpit*, Edinburgh, 1927, pp. 202-212.

The Free Church Presbytery of Inverness hear with gratification that the Free North Church congregation of Inverness have attained their centenary as a congregation. They extend to all the office-bearers, communicants and adherents in the congregation their warmest good wishes, thanking God for His great mercy in having continued the Gospel witness in these parts, for having vouchsafed blessings as great and many, for having provided a succession of gracious ministers and generations of faithful men and women. They pray that Divine favour may continue to rest on the congregation, that glorious things may be spoken of it, and that of many Heaven's Record may tell – 'this man was born there.'

They rejoice in the Lord that the congregation's care in the work of the Lord at home and abroad has always flourished, and that they have communicated with, and strengthened other congregations, as they remembered them suffering adversity. Whilst commending their past good works, the Presbytery take this occasion to exhort to still greater works, and that, in full consciousness of their being put in trust with the Gospel, and in knowledge of their inheriting a glorious heritage, the rising generation may study well the sacrifices and testimony of their fathers, and know that the Free Church has a witness much needed today – a testimony all should feel honoured to uphold by regular attendance at the means of Grace, and by loving and spontaneous sacrifice to the Cause and Kingdom of Messiah. 'Watch ye, stand fast in the faith, quit you like men, be strong.' In the name of the Free Church Presbytery,

Signed, James Irvine, Moderator.

At this time Mr. Cameron also received the following communication from the Kirk Session of St Columba High Church, Inverness:

Rev. and Dear Sir, –

At a meeting of the Kirk Session held last night, special mention was made of the Free North Church and your congregation's centenary. I am requested to write and convey to you and your Session the hearty congratulations of this Session on your having attained your centenary as a congregation.

Yours very sincerely,

Alexr. W. Fraser.

These gracious tributes were noted and suitably acknowledged.

Mr. Cameron's scholarly ability was recognised throughout the Free Church and his name was forwarded with others for the Chair of Greek and New Testament Studies in the Free Church College. But he withdrew it, and in the Kirk Session minute of June, 1937, the Free North Session expressed their pleasure that he had done so. They took the opportunity of assuring him that they highly valued his services and hoped that he would long be spared to go in and out among them.

He had a brother and two sisters. Angus died in 1935. His sister, Margaret, was a school teacher who passed away in 1970. Another sister, Miss Elizabeth, spent many years in Craig Dunain Hospital, and died in 1987. She was a dear old lady who was frequently visited by the older generation of the Church. She never lost her interest in the congregation that meant much to her, and invariably her parting words to her minister after a visit were, "The Lord bless you and give you souls for your hire."

The congregation in the 1930s was still of considerable size and it had a large and well attended Sunday School. The annual soirée and summer outing for young folks were still held. The young men's Mutual Improvement Society, and the girls Sewing Class were replaced by a Youth Fellowship. There seems to have been a spiritual quickening among the young people in the late twenties and early thirties when a number of them became members and bright witnesses for Christ. John MacPherson who was associated with the congregation became minister of Ayr Free Church in 1935 and then of Creich in 1946. He also served as a chaplain in the armed forces during the second world war. William R. Mackay became minister successively of Duthil 1937-46, Buccleuch and Greyfriars 1946-49, Kingussie and Alvie 1949-61, and was appointed Chaplain to Inverness Hospitals 1961-77. He also served as a Chaplain to the Forces during the war years. Donald F. Mackenzie, Culduthel Road, and Charles T. Rose of Lochalsh Road, became students for the ministry but there is no record of whether they eventually became ministers of the gospel. After war service, Duncan G. W. Beaton studied at the Free Church College and became minister of Ayr Free Church, 1952-60, and the Free Church, Leith, 1960-82. These were all young men who attended the Free North in the thirties and were influenced by the gospel.

At the beginning of 1937 a request was made by a number of young people for the use of the upper vestry where they could meet from time to time for prayer and Bible study. They also "desired to engage in aggressive [evangelical] work in certain districts of the town, for example holding cottage meetings of an evangelistic nature." The Kirk Session after deliberation came to the following finding: "(1) They welcome your zeal and devotion. (2) They have no objections to your holding kitchen meetings, provided the people are agreeable. (3) They agree to give you the use of the upper Session Room for one night weekly, either on a Monday or a Thursday. (4) They would like an elder to be with you on the occasions you meet for prayer and reading of the Word of God. (5) They expect that the mode of worship will be that which is recognised by the Word of God and the church to which we belong. (6) They are glad that you are hoping to do aggressive evangelistic work, and they look upon the mission in which we are interested, and where you already have been, as an admirable field for such work. (7) And they hope that the stated services of the church on Sabbath and the weekly prayer meeting will find you regularly there. (8) And having thus granted you a place of meeting, they think that your going to other places should now cease." Some thought the restrictions too severe and expressed their disappointment with the session's response. It is undoubtedly necessary to direct wisely the enthusiasm of young Christians, but care must be taken not to extinguish the zeal and optimism of youth.

As the decade drew to a close there were ominous signs that Europe was again to be engulfed in war. Germany annexed Austria and Slovakia and claimed the Danzig Corridor in Poland. Britain and France resolved to withstand the aggressor. Soon a *blitzkrieg* was underway when the mighty Panzer Divisions of the Third Reich swept everything before them.

In the East Poland was overrun. In the West everything fell to the victorious German armies as they swept to the Channel ports. A long and wearisome war in Europe now had to be fought which was to last from September, 1939, until May, 1945. The Church was again decimated as young men and women became involved in the conflict. Some were never to return to the congregation, either through death, or marrying and settling down in other places.

During those war years all buildings had to be darkened to prevent enemy air attacks. To completely black out a building the size of the Free North Church would have been at prohibitive cost, so services were continued in the Church in the forenoon and in the hall in the evening.

Throughout the War years Mr. Cameron preached to and visited his people as before. But the years were beginning to take their toll. In 1938 he had been laid aside from his duties through illness. Then the strain and burden of two heavy charges extending over a period of 30 years began to tell. After 43 years in the ministry, he decided that the time had come to lay down the burden and hand it over to a successor. In 1945 he retired and went to live in a house that had been purchased in Burghead where he and Mrs Cameron spent the rest of their days. He died in 1947, at the age of 70, and his body was laid to rest in Burghead cemetery. Mrs Cameron passed away in 1957, and her body rests beside that of her husband.

In the August issue of the Free Church *Monthly Record* for 1947, the Rev. Kenneth A. MacRae pays his predecessor a fine and well-merited tribute. Speaking of Mr Cameron's Stornoway ministry, he says, "By the time of his settlement in his new charge, Mr. Cameron had attained to the full maturity of his powers and his 16 years ministry in Stornoway was fraught with blessing. Undoubtedly this period was the richest of his career. A first-class theologian, a careful and exact student, a deeply experimental preacher and an indefatigable pastor, he speedily won for himself a unique place in the religious life of the island. In his preaching he had a sweet, wooing note which made a wonderful appeal to the Lord's people, while the clear, terse and well-arranged structure of his sermons, wherein no such thing as tediousness was ever suffered to appear, made him a preacher whom the younger element heard gladly." Such a ministry was also carried on in the Free North in Inverness.

Mr. MacRae goes on to say, "Mr. Cameron was a deeply exercised man of God and therein lay the secret of his power as a preacher. Too often it is only when a man is gone that his true value comes to be realised. In this case it is very evident that Mr Cameron's gifts, abilities and usefulness never received – even within his own church – the recognition which were their due. A great man was among us and we knew it not."

CHAPTER 6

DONALD CAMPBELL

IT WAS HOPED that after Mr Cameron's retirement there would be a speedy settlement, but instead five troublesome years were to elapse before a new minister was inducted.

When the vacancy began there existed harmony and goodwill among the people. In the immediate post-war years, the Rev. Murray Macleod, who was at home on furlough from Chhapara in India, rendered valuable service in the Inverness pulpit. Later, the Rev. J. Calvin Mackay, who had settled in the town after mission service in Lima, also gave considerable help to the congregation. The services of these men were greatly appreciated.

Malcolm Murray Macleod belonged to Dunoon and was born of Isle of Lewis parents. He became a student at the Free Church College in Edinburgh around 1930. Dr Anne Urquhart tells us that it was while listening to an address given by Miss Elizabeth Macleod to the Free Church Students Missionary Society that he was influenced to proceed to Central Province in India as a preacher of the gospel. Miss Macleod was a daughter of the manse. Her father was one of the 26 ministers who remained in the Free Church after the union in 1900. She went to India in 1905 as a Biblewoman and apart from furloughs remained there until

1948. Miss Elizabeth Macleod was a highly respected missionary lady and after her retirement from India she came to Edinburgh to live with her sister. She, along with Miss Catherine, was always to be seen in their place of worship in Free St Columba's in Edinburgh.

Murray Macleod who had been influenced by her to work in India, married Sarah Morrison, a trained nurse, and in 1933 they went to Lakhnadon. In her book *Near India's Heart*, Dr Urquhart informs us that he "had an excellent grasp of Hindi and was highly thought of by Indian and Scottish colleagues."[54] She also informs us that it was when "Learning about Hinduism, he became disturbed by similarities between infant baptism and a Hindu rite which confirmed tiny children in their caste. He corresponded with several prominent Free Churchmen about this and continued his study on the subject during home leave. When, in the early forties, he became convinced that infant baptism was not biblical, he offered to resign. Wartime conditions made replacement difficult. At the request of the Foreign Missions Committee, he continued in the ministry at Lakhnadon and Chhapara, neither pressing his Baptist views on others nor baptising infants."[55] In 1949 he pastored Union Church in Ootacamund, a South Indian hill resort. On his return to Scotland he became a Baptist minister and was called to Harper Memorial Church in Glasgow. He then went to Canada and for twelve years lectured in New Testament Exegesis and Missions at Toronto Bible College. The Macleods settled in Ontario where they lived in retirement, and there they passed on to be with Christ the Saviour.

It was during his furlough in 1946 that Murray Macleod came to stay in Inverness. He was then in his prime and was invited to take the oversight of the Free North pulpit. His charismatic personality made a great impression upon the people and particularly the young. Miss Nan Macdonald who was then a teenager in the congregation speaks of his dynamic ministry and his gift of communication. The young men and

---

[54] Anne M. Urquhart, *Near India's Heart*, Edinburgh, 1990, pp. 60.
[55] As above, p. 61.

women who had been on war service were now returning home and on 15th May, 1947, a 'Welcome Home' gathering took place. It was chaired by Mr A. S. Fraser the Session Clerk. After the meal there was a reception when Mr and Mrs Murray Macleod took part along with the Provost of the town, Mr Hugh Ross, and the following ministers, W. R. Mackay of the Free Church, R. Murchison of the Church of Scotland, and John MacBeath of the Baptist Church. Presentation Bibles were given to those who had been on active war service. All too soon the Rev. Murray Macleod's furlough expired and he returned to India.

The other missionary who gave invaluable service to the congregation was the Rev. John Calvin Mackay. He began his ministry in the Free Church in Nairn in 1915. The call to missionary work in Peru was irresistible and in 1919 he left for Cajamarca where in the midst of difficulties, opposition, and danger to himself and his family he diligently laboured in His Master's service. After a serious accident he returned home in 1934 and on his recovery was settled as minister at Kincardine and Croick in 1938. On an urgent call from the Church, he returned to Peru in 1945 and served as acting Headmaster at Colegio San Andrés in Lima until 1947. He returned to Inverness and was appointed Hospitals' Chaplain. Like Murray Macleod he too gave whatever help he could. He was a loyal and faithful member and elder of the congregation until his death in 1985. He was indeed a gracious man of God and as the Peruvians called him, 'el caballero cristiano' (the Christian gentleman).[56]

Meanwhile efforts were made to secure a successor to Mr Cameron and approaches were made to some of the best-known Free Church ministers of the day but to no avail. In 1947, Rev. Hector MacRury, of Gairloch, was invited to preach. He was a Glasgow Highlander whose parents came from North Uist, and being a bi-lingual preacher he had what was required for the charge. Indeed, there were those among his contemporaries who regarded his preaching gifts as exceptional and his congregation in Gairloch who esteemed him highly would have been

---

[56] John M. MacPherson, *At the Roots of a Nation*, Edinburgh, 1993, p. 89.

reluctant to part with him. He had gone to Gairloch in Wester Ross in 1935 and now had ten years of experience in the ministry. To begin with there was cordiality about proceeding with a call and necessary steps were taken, but problems arose which were to have disastrous results on the unity of the congregation. Two sides with deeply entrenched attitudes emerged and bitterness was engendered so that a split in the congregation seemed inevitable. The matter went through the courts of the Church and eventually the General Assembly instructed the congregation to begin again and that Mr MacRury's name be dropped.

During this period of unrest the congregation suffered a serious haemorrhage when disaffected and embittered members and adherents left the congregation, and there being no other Free Church in the vicinity they made their way to other places of worship in the town. They never returned, and sometimes their descendants at Free North funerals or weddings would speak of their parents or grandparents who once belonged to the North Church. It was 1950 before a new minister was settled in Inverness Free Church.

Donald Murdo Campbell was born in Lower Bayble, Point, Lewis, on 7th February, 1913. He was the seventh son and in those days there was a superstitious belief that such a person was able to cure what was known as 'king's evil' by putting his hands on the neck of the sufferer. This was a custom he disliked intensely and when anyone came to his home for that purpose, he made himself scarce until they were gone. His parents died when he was sixteen and a sister took over the duties of the home.

His wife Mabel has informed me that he came to Christ as his Saviour in early manhood when he was "awakened by fear of the second coming of Christ and his unpreparedness for judgment." It was in Jesus the Saviour that he found peace for his stricken conscience and rest for his troubled soul. When he appeared before the Kirk Session for admission to the Lord's Table he had been seeking a sign that would be a mark of grace and confirm his faith when God's word spoke to him. "No sign shall be given but the sign of the prophet Jonah." He was made to understand that he was to rest his hope for eternity not on signs but only on the death and resurrection of Christ Jesus and nothing else.

In his youth he went to Glasgow and began work in the engineering department of a Clydeside shipyard. During those days he worshipped in Govan Free Church whose minister was the Rev. Alexander Macleod who pastored Govan from 1938 to 1947, and then Back, in Lewis, from 1947 to 1954. He was the father of Rev. M. A. Macleod of Stornoway. While in Glasgow Mr Campbell felt the call to preach the gospel, and so he commenced studies at the Bible Training Institute. His intention was to become a missionary with The *Regions Beyond Missionary Union*, but the call to the ministry of the Free Church became irresistible. To attain the academic standard for entrance to the Free Church College he moved to Edinburgh to study at Skerry's College. It was in the Elementary Latin Class that he met the gracious and gifted young lady tutor who became his wife. They were married on 1st July, 1946.

After completing studies for the ministry of the Free Church, Mr. Campbell was called to Milton Free Church, in Cowcaddens, in the heart of the city of Glasgow. Milton held a distinguished place in the annals of Free Church history. In recent years due to diminishing numbers it was linked to St Vincent Street Free Church and the old building has now been demolished. In October, 1949, he was inducted to the charge and here his ministry began and although it lasted for only a short time we believe that it was not unfruitful. The following year the Inverness congregation elected him to fill the vacancy and he was inducted to the Free North in January 1951. The text that prompted him to accept the challenge of Inverness, was Acts chapter 18, verse 10: "I am with thee, and no man shall set on thee to hurt thee, for I have much people in this city."

When he arrived in Inverness the Free North congregation was still divided. Old wounds were unhealed and it was difficult for him to feel accepted by those who, in one way or another, made it obvious that he was not the man of their choice. On the other hand, there were loyal and welcoming people who readily extended to him the hand of friendship.

A few years later, however, an event that was to have an adverse effect upon the North Church was the emergence of Free Greyfriars congregation in 1957.

The Church building, 'St Mary's', at the end of Church Street, is only a few hundred yards from the Free North. It was the Gaelic charge of the Church of Scotland. In the 1940s the congregation was no longer essentially Gaelic and being almost adjacent to the High Church was asked to relocate to the new housing development scheme at Dalneigh on the west side of the river Ness. The Church of Scotland sold 'St Mary's' building as a place of worship to the Rev. Ewen MacQueen and his supporters who had become disaffected from the Free Presbyterian Church over an internal dispute. When Mr MacQueen died, he was succeeded by Rev. Alexander Macleod. After he resigned, the MacQueen Memorial congregation in 1956 agreed to petition the Free Church of Scotland to be accepted as a Free Church congregation with the right to call a minister of their choice. The request of the petition was granted but with a proviso which appears in the Inverness Free Church Presbytery Records and which reads, "That in view of the proximity of the MacQueen Memorial Church to the Free North, and to promote the best interests of both congregations, provision be made for a review of the whole situation as affecting the future development of these two congregations respecting the question of Church extension in the Burgh of Inverness."

The new congregation proceeded to call Rev. Donald Macdonald, minister at Urray in Ross-shire, and in 1958 Mr. Macdonald was inducted to the charge. The Church was renamed Free Greyfriars. Mr Macdonald came from Lewis and was a popular choice and served with success the Greyfriars congregation until his death in 1977. Those in the Free North who still felt aggrieved at what had happened in the immediate post war years joined Greyfriars and some Free Church families coming to live in the town attached themselves to the new congregation. It was in the early 1990s that Greyfriars relocated to a new redevelopment housing area in the Hilton district of the town and erected a purpose-built church on Balloan Road.

For a young man beginning his ministry, the task before Mr Campbell was daunting. People defecting from his congregation through no fault on his part, and the emergence of another Free Church on the doorstep of the Free North must have been hard to bear. However, he was given grace and fortitude to carry on in the face of difficulties. He applied himself to the work of proclaiming faithfully the gospel of Christ and addressed its invitation to sinners with a wooing appeal. He gave himself diligently to the task of pastoring his people and in time

Rev. Donald Campbell

he secured a warm place in their affections and loyalty. He was a man of peace and with the passing of time wounds were healed and he was used in bringing souls to a knowledge of the saving grace of God in Christ the Saviour.

I remember him from student days in the Free Church College. He was his own man. I recall him preaching in the late 1940s in the hall of the old Greenock Free Church. His theme was 'Calvary' and the words of his text were from Matthew chapter 27, verse 36: "And sitting down they watched him there." After describing the different groups of people who gathered round the Cross to watch the suffering Saviour and describing their different reactions, he personalised the scene and applied it to his audience. More than half a century has passed since then but his earnestness in the pulpit is before me and the way he introduced the striking words of Horatius Bonar,

> I see the crowd in Pilate's hall I mark their wrathful mien;
> Their shouts of 'Crucify' appal, with blasphemy between.
> And of that shouting multitude I feel that I am one;
> And in that din of voices rude I recognise my own.
> I see the scourges tear His back, I see the piercing crown;
> And of that crowd who smite and mock, I feel that I am one.

Around yon cross the throng I see, mocking the Sufferer's groan:
Yet still my voice it seems to be, as if I mocked alone.
'Twas I that shed the sacred blood, I nailed him to the tree,
I crucified the Christ of God, I joined the mockery.
Yet not the less that blood avails to cleanse away my sin,
And not the less that cross prevails to give me peace within.

Another sermon I recall him preaching was the Saturday preparatory service in the early 1960s when we were assisting at Lochinver communion. His text was a familiar one for such an occasion. It was from Mark chapter 14, verse 15: "And he will shew you a large upper room furnished and prepared: there make ready for us." His points were, the largeness of the room being indicative of the mercy of God, the preparation made for the guests, and the need for the guests being prepared for the feast.

In his days in the Free North, the Sabbath Gaelic service was held immediately after the forenoon English, in the upper session room. The Gaelic people referred to this room as 'The Upper Room,' and here in his native tongue he often excelled in Gaelic preaching. Mr Donald Campbell, the Gaelic elder, on one occasion before his death, was regaling me with some stories of bye-gone days. He told me how Mr Campbell was preaching on Paul praying for the removal of the thorn in the flesh. In Gaelic, he said, "No, Paul, you carry the thorn, but I'll carry you and the thorn." It was at that time Mr Campbell told me of Mr Duncan MacLennan whom it was my privilege to know as one of my elders. He was a devout Gaelic elder who came from Harris and who prayed with his arms held up. Donald smiled as he told me how in his own quaint way in Gaelic Mr MacLennan said, "If it would be a hen house we live in, it would be a palace if you yourself were there." Mr MacLennan and his wife used to have Gaelic worship, morning, noon, and night, each day. When he died, the late Rev. Donald Macdonald of Greyfriars, who shared in the funeral service, said to me, when we left the pulpit, "You will miss his prayers." Such likeminded prayerful men and women who have gone to their reward leave the Church on earth the poorer without them.

Mr Campbell had his hobbies such as fishing on some loch with Rev. John Murdo Macleod the Church's Evangelist, or Mr Archie MacArthur a deacon of the Free North, men who were equally keen on fishing. He had a good voice and enjoyed singing the beautiful and moving Gaelic hymns. Another interest, stemming from his days as an engineer was cars. He enjoyed browsing in second hand theological book shops and acquired a large and choice library.

Mr Campbell was in his prime when he passed on to be with His Saviour. He suffered a heart attack in 1967 when he was only 54 years old. He passed peacefully away in Inverness on 17th October, 1967. His funeral was from his Church, and his remains were interred in Tomnahurich cemetery. His wife has informed me that he had great assurance on his death bed and quoted the words, "I know that my Redeemer liveth," and "His blood covers all my sins."

Professor Roderick A. Finlayson, who conducted the funeral service, said that the Church at large thought Mr Campbell was not the right choice, but had to admit subsequently that they were wrong. He was a man of peace and as such he was able to bind together a divided congregation.

That is what the Rev. D. M. Campbell was: a man of peace. In the obituary which appeared in the December issue of *The Monthly Record* for 1967 it says, "Mr Campbell was of an unassuming and peaceable nature, and one who 'esteemed others better than himself.'" It goes on to say this: "Although he did not take a prominent part in the deliberations of Church courts, his was always a gracious influence. He served for a period on the Standing committees of the Church. He gave a period of service to the Canadian field ministering at the Highland Church, Vancouver." The obituary, signed A.G., whom we presume was the late Rev. Alasdair Gollan, a fellow student, a friend, and a co-Presbyter, continues: "A persuasive and winsome preacher in both Gaelic and English, it was his constant aim and delight to point sinners to his Lord and Saviour in the glory of His Person and in the all-sufficiency of His atoning work. To his congregation Mr Campbell was a sympathetic and understanding pastor.

He showed a special interest in young people who came to work or study in Inverness. They found in him a true shepherd of souls. Like his Master, he often went in search of the sheep that had gone astray, for 'his heart's desire and prayer to God for them was that they might be saved'. He endeared himself to his congregation, and he was supremely happy in their midst. Unswerving in his loyalty to the doctrinal standards of his Church, Mr Campbell had a charitable outlook upon the whole household of Faith."

CHAPTER 7

JAMES FRASER

JAMES WILLIAM FRASER was born in Milton, Glenurquhart, on 15 May, 1914, the fourth son (in a family of 4 sons and 1 daughter) of Andrew Fraser and his wife Elizabeth MacCallum, both natives of the Glen. It was a time of ecclesiastical turmoil caused by the union of the majority of the Free Church with the United Presbyterian Church in 1900. Communities, even families, were divided. James' parents went into the union and he was baptised in the United Free Church. In 1921 he lost his father as a result of an accident that brought on paralysis and less than a year later his mother died of cancer. The young family was looked after by their maternal aunts and the three youngest went to live with their maternal grandparents. In this way the whole family were brought up in the Free Church. At this time Glenurquhart was in a transition period from a predominating Gaelic culture. The youngsters were taught the *Shorter Catechism* in Gaelic and were certainly in a bilingual situation.

James Fraser was a diligent student as a succession of prize books from Glenurquhart Higher Grade school testifies. He was dux of the primary school in 1927 and of the secondary school in 1933. He was particularly good at English becoming one of the top three passes for the whole of Scotland in Higher English for that year. He learned discipline and the good stewardship of time and talents. The orphan boy was expected to take part in the everyday work of a small croft. Here he learned basics that were to stand him in good stead as minister of Plockton and Kyle. He got from one of his aunts a love of gardening and beekeeping which followed him throughout his life.

From school James proceeded to Edinburgh University via the Bursary competition. There he had two professors highly respected in the academic world Professor Grierson in the English department and Professor W. J. Watson (author of *The Celtic Place-Names of Scotland* [1926]). It may be worth noting that James Fraser won the class medal of his year in the Celtic Class. In those days there was a lively and stimulating Free Church Students Association where he enjoyed the company of like-minded students. He attended St Columba's Free Church where he became a communicant then enjoying the ministry of Alexander Stewart, D.D., a native of Sutherland who preached Gaelic and English with a warm heart and a cultured Biblical emphasis. Dr Stewart's style of preaching had a strong influence on James as well as others who later entered the ministry. After graduating M.A., James Fraser proceeded to the Free Church College where he developed a love for the Hebrew Scriptures and had the privilege of having Edmund K. Simpson as lecturer in Greek and New Testament. During his time in Edinburgh, James had the benefit of the hospitable home of James Macdonald from Glenurquhart, an elder in St Columba's. At that time began a lifetime friendship with an older student, James Mackintosh, whose roots were in 'the Glen' and Ferintosh. Student days were happy days. During these years his minister at home was Rev. Ewen MacRury (a native of North Uist) from 1925-1935 and Rev. Farquhar Matheson (a native of Plockton) from 1936. Mr MacRury once remarked to a fellow minister: "I have two bright boys in my congregation; James Fraser and Clement Graham." He was not to be disappointed in them. It was in Edinburgh that James Fraser first professed faith as a communicant member.

James Fraser having completed his college course was duly licensed to preach the gospel. Martyrs Free Church, Wick, was originally a

Reformed Presbyterian congregation which came into the Free Church in the union of 1876. The first minister of Martyrs Free Church was Finlay Munro Harper, who was inducted there in 1877. He went into the United Free Church in 1900. The remnant Free Church was adjudicated the church (known locally as Finlay Harper's) but had a long vacancy, until James W Fraser was ordained and inducted in 1938. And here he served right through the War years. These were years of coming and going of military personnel. Wick was even bombed but without serious damage. Mr Fraser was an Air-raid Warden during that time. Caithness was very different from Glenurquhart and the Caithness people from the Glen folk but in the course of 10 years ministry there James Fraser formed a high opinion of the Caithness Christian. No doubt the straight-forward character of the people appealed to his own straight and honest character. He often spoke of some of the godly Caithness men and women he was privileged to have known those early years.

In July, 1943, James Fraser married Margaret Mae Cameron from Allanglach, Knockbain. They had been contemporaries in Edinburgh where she was a student in the University and later Moray House Teacher Training College. Margaret Cameron, known to family and friends as Margot, taught in Drumsmittal, Ardgay and Ferintosh before her marriage. As a farmer's daughter she brought her skills to good use during the Plockton and Kyle years. Allanglach farm was known far and wide among the 'gentlemen of the road' as a place where they would find shelter in the barn and a good meal. Margot Cameron, as Mrs Fraser, continued this kindly sympathy with the unfortunate. Down the years many from various walks of life had warm memories of the manse hospitality of the Frasers in their various congregations.

During the Wick years James and Margot had three boys and one girl who was only three years old when the call to Plockton and Kyle took them to a new sphere of ministry. The Wick years were succeeded by a ministry in which the full powers of mind and body were stretched almost to their limit. The couple were in their prime of life when this move came. God makes no mistakes.

In December, 1948, James Fraser was translated to this large congregation comprising Plockton and Kyle with the villages between, together with Stromeferry and its adjacent townships. The call had 213 names. It was a new situation for the young minister. He now had a Gaelic service in Plockton at 12.30 and an earlier English service in Kyle at 11am. There was an English service in Plockton at 5pm followed by another at 6.30pm in Kyle. As the manse was in Plockton these services involved 28 miles back and fore on a very narrow single track. This was not all. Every month there was an afternoon (3pm) service in Stromeferry which involved a 24-mile return trip via Auchtertyre. There was also a service once a month at 3pm in Duncraig Castle College attended by girls from all parts of the Highlands (including Lewis) who were taking the domestic science course. This made the preaching responsibility for these days 5 services. It was a gruelling schedule. The Gaelic services were to begin with heavy going. He used to say that having had to learn the Gaelic *Shorter Catechism* in his grandparent's home was an excellent preparation for the theological vocabulary required. There were prayer meetings in the villages during the week as well as in Plockton and Kyle. In those days Duirinish, Drumbuie and Erbusaig were vibrant Gaelic communities. The Glenurquhart boyhood helped, as many of the household visits were among the older generation.

Mrs Fraser had her hands full with five little children but was taken into the hearts of the Plockton people. She was highly respected for her kindness and interest in the youngsters of the village. After some years it seemed a good idea to get a cow – milk was brought from Dingwall, not always fresh, as well as being dear. The minister's salary was barely adequate so the cow entered the scene. Now there was fresh milk, butter and crowdie. The croft/glebe was able to provide not only hay and straw for the cow but also potatoes and turnips. Mr Fraser was a progressive crofter whose skill with the scythe was something of a byword in the village. There is no doubt that this aspect of his ministry earned him respect in the community. One Free Presbyterian said. "He hasn't got a lazy bone in his body". Both minister and wife milked the cow and many a bottle of milk was given away to neighbours. The most obvious fruit of hard work and practical knowledge was the manse garden – fruitful in blackcurrants, strawberries, raspberries, productive in table vegetables and a delight to the eye of all who appreciated beauty. Mr Fraser took a full part in the life of the village. One winter, art class; and another winter, woodwork. He built by himself a large deep-litter shed for the hens. Not only was James Fraser a practical man he was also a man of outstanding academic ability.

During his ministry in Plockton he studied for the London B.D. which he duly obtained. His pulpit preparation was meticulous. A knowledge of the Hebrew and Greek Scriptures guided his thinking. The Scriptures as the Word of God were his theological touchstone. Indeed, until almost the very end of his life, he read daily from the Hebrew Scriptures. There was nothing slipshod in anything he set his hand or mind to. It was during his ministry in Plockton and Kyle that he was called to serve for six months in the Vancouver congregation, from whence he brought back the idea of church camps, which he imported into the Free Church, persevering with it even after more than one setback at the General Assembly. It was also while in Plockton that he became editor of the *Instructor*, initiating many changes to its content and style. You might ask how any man could have coped with such a busy life and yet not at the expense of his congregational duties. Perhaps the answer is that he had a strong physical and mental constitution – above the ordinary. It also helped that he never wasted time. If there was something to be done he did it "yesterday if not sooner", as he once said to a member of the family who asked when did he want him to do a certain job. All that he was engaged in was in the service of his Saviour and nothing was too menial as his favourite poet George Herbert said (and he often quoted it): "Who sweeps a room as for thy laws…Makes that and the action fine."

Such a busy life could not have been possible without the like-minded support of a helpmeet who could turn her hands to such varied tasks as milking the cow and teaching a Bible Class (and for a time teaching in the Secondary school) as well as being a mother much loved by her children.

Her hospitality was greatly appreciated by the regular visitors from the Mission to Lepers, the National Bible Society of Scotland, the Unevangelised Fields Mission, the British Jews Society (later Christian Witness to Israel and currently International Mission to Jewish People) and the China Inland Mission (now Overseas Missionary Fellowship). Margaret Fraser was deeply interested in foreign missionary work, as also her husband James, who was many years a member of the Christian Witness to Israel board as well as convener of the Free Church Foreign Missions Board.

There was a core of exercised Christians in the congregation who upheld the minister and his wife in prayer. The Lord moves his servants as he sees need in his church. It was with a feeling of sadness that the family left Plockton in April, 1960. Margaret (Mrs Fraser) was unable to take a full part in the flitting. Her health was beginning to suffer from a demanding life. God saw a move was necessary.

In April, 1960, Rev. James W Fraser was inducted to the charge of Free Buccleuch and Greyfriars, Edinburgh. Although a small congregation as city charges go (the call had 103 names on it) it had a long history. The handsome church, with its tall spire, is the only Edinburgh Free Church building to have remained with its congregation from the Disruption. Built in 1865 for the congregation who followed their minister, Rev. Patrick Clason, out of St Cuthbert's Chapel of Ease (Buccleuch). Patrick Clason was joint Assembly Clerk from 1843-1867. In 1897 the congregation of Free Greyfriars with their minister Rev. Donald M. Macalister were united with Free Buccleuch. In 1900 both ministers Robert Gordon (Buccleuch) and D. M. Macalister (Greyfriars) did not join the Union.

When James Fraser came to Buccleuch & Greyfriars, Professor Roderick A. Finlayson and Professor William J. Cameron of the Free Church College were elders. The lowland heritage was strong. The majority were Edinburgh folk although this slowly changed as others – students, nurses – found the congregation congenial and the preaching instructive. It was a big change from the hectic ministry in Plockton and Kyle. In Buccleuch there were the normal two Sunday services and the weekly prayer meeting. During this time Mr Fraser moved from editor of *The Instructor* to editor of *The Monthly Record*. He followed Dr A. M. Renwick as visiting Church History lecturer in the Faith Mission College. As a result, some of the students worshipped in Buccleuch. He was Free Church representative on the Scottish Education Committee (where he often found support for his uncompromising stand for Christian values from the Roman Catholic member). He continued his work on the Foreign Missions Committee and as Free Church representative on the Christian Witness to Israel board.

After the evening service there was an opportunity for the young folk to ask questions at the Bible Class. This was appreciated by some foreign students, the two most notable being from Holland and Greece. Of those who attended Buccleuch in their student days some went to the Indian mission and some to Peru and South Africa. James Fraser had a broad vision of the worldwide church. In this he was assisted by the hospitality of the manse. Mrs Fraser was a mother in Israel. The manse was open to all who wished to come. Apart from the Free Church students there were some unusual ones who, having come to the church, found themselves invited to a meal in the manse. One year a group of Armenian teachers from the diaspora in Lebanon were on a course in Edinburgh. The manse family was augmented for a few months by two boys from Colegio San Andrés in Lima, Peru. Although the congregational pressures were less than in Plockton and Kyle, Mr Fraser continued his pastoral visitation. The manse garden was small but continued to produce vegetables as well as flowers. A favourite relaxation was going for a run to the Borders – very close to South Edinburgh – out on the Biggar road. During this time James Fraser was interim-moderator of London Free Church congregation. In 1965 he was moderator of the Free Church General Assembly.

In December 1968, Mr Fraser was inducted to the charge of the Free North, Inverness. It was in one way a home-going for the Glenurquhart boy and Black Isle girl. This was his last pastoral charge, to which he brought the experience of thirty years in the ministry. But here he

Rev. James Fraser

experienced the loss of his wife, Margot, in 1970, whose health had been overwhelmed by her busy life of service to others. This was followed shortly after by the death of his elder daughter, Elspeth, who had come home from New Zealand suffering from melanoma. This was a heavy blow which he felt deeply but bore with Christian fortitude as the will of his Father in heaven. Margot had always believed he needed the support of an helpmeet and hoped on her death he would remarry. It was not an easy place to fill but James Fraser found a true helpmeet in Mabel Cumming, widow of Rev. D. M. Campbell, his predecessor. Mabel knew the congregation well and her return to the manse was a great help. In the Free North, Mr Fraser took a Gaelic service as well as the morning and evening English services and a Gaelic prayer meeting before the English prayer meeting on Wednesdays. Weddings are a part of every ministry but the Free North, being central and having a wonderful set of steps at the front for photographing large wedding groups, Mr Fraser was kept busy in that respect. He had a gift of setting people at their ease in such situations. Never confusing humour with playing the clown, he used his native wit in a way that exercised a positive influence on the company.

During his time in the Free North, James Fraser demonstrated his ability as an able Bible teacher. His sermons were always clear, well organised, interesting and memorable. Those who heard him preach can still remember his sermons even after the passage of 50 years. Preaching from Revelation chapter 1, verse 7 ("Behold he cometh with clouds; and every eye shall see him: and they also which pierced him: and all kindreds [tribes] of the earth will wail [mourn] because of him. Even so, Amen") he introduced the sermon by referring to the then recent Apollo landing on the Moon which was watched by millions all over the world. His two main headings were that the personal return of Christ is: (1) A sure and decisive event and (2) A glorious and stimulating hope. One young hearer at the time recalls him quoting on a number of occasions the opening words of Horatius Bonar's hymn: 'Upon a life I have not lived, Upon a death I did not die, Another's life, Another's Death, I stake my whole eternity'.

It is probably true to say that the years in the Free North were the mature outcome of his previous ministries. James Fraser loved preaching the Word of God in its breadth and depth and so it was with a certain regret that he accepted as his duty the post of Professor of Old Testament Language and Literature in the Free Church College to which he was appointed by the General Assembly in 1974. In those days the professors were not only teachers of their subject but also the guides and advisors of future ministers. James Fraser had a wealth of experience in the pastoral ministry. He retired in 1983 after being diagnosed in February with bowel cancer (the cause of his mother's death). In November 1983, a life of unstinted service to his Lord and Saviour came to a close. "Blessed are the dead who die in the Lord from henceforth: Yea, saith the Spirit, that they may rest from their labours; and their works do follow them" (Revelation 14:13).

Apart from his involvement with the denominational magazines, Mr Fraser did not write much. He did, however, produce a booklet for the Free Church on *Marriage is God's Way* in 1968, and he contributed a chapter on 'The Ordination of Women,' in *Hold Fast Your Confession*, a collection of studies in Church Principles produce by the Knox Press in 1978.

THE AUTHOR

The Rev. Hugh M. Ferrier was born in Greenock on the 11th June, 1925, to Isle of Harris parents, and was the youngest of six children. He professed saving faith in Christ in 1943. In 1953 Mr Ferrier married Georgina (Georet) Cameron, daughter of the Rev. William Cameron, Resolis.

Rev. H.M. Ferrier M.A. 1975 - 1990

Ordained and inducted to Golspie Free Church in 1952, Mr Ferrier was called to Knockbain in 1960, to Partick, Crow Road, Glasgow, in 1963, and to his final charge of Inverness Free North in 1975. He retired from that pastorate on account of ill health in 1990. He was Moderator of the General Assembly of the Free Church of Scotland in 1978.

Mr Ferrier adhered to the Free Church of Scotland (Continuing) in 2000. In 2006 that Church published his major work, *Echoes from Scotland's Heritage of Grace*. It covers incidents and movements in the history of the Church in Scotland from Reformation times. In his Preface he wrote: "I have written these pages to try to express some of the glories of God's grace experienced by Scottish people in the past." This present book, produced posthumously, reflects the same concern, as the author deals with the faithful works and ministries of Inverness Free North ministers in the past, up to the time of his predecessor in that charge.

Mr Ferrier continued to preach up to 2009. He fell asleep in Jesus on 5th December, 2013, and his funeral service was held in the Free North Church, which he had served so faithfully. Hugh Ferrier was a man of strong Biblical evangelical and reformation principles, but a man of a warm and gracious disposition. He was an engaging and faithful preacher of the Word, a diligent pastor, a man of God, and one for whom it was evident that Christ was all. (Revelation 14:12-13).

Free Church of Scotland General Assembly,
Free North Church, Inverness, May 1922.